THOMAS JEFFERSON ON LEADERSHIP

For Walker,
the history buff &
aspiring CEO.
Dad '03

THOMAS JEFFERSON ON LEADERSHIP

EXECUTIVE LESSONS FROM HIS LIFE AND LETTERS

COY BAREFOOT

A PLUME BOOK

PLUME
Published by the Penguin Group
Penguin Putnam Inc., 375 Hudson Street,
New York, New York 10014, U.S.A.
Penguin Books Ltd, 80 Strand,
London WC2R 0RL England
Penguin Books Australia Ltd, Ringwood,
Victoria, Australia
Penguin Books Canada Ltd, 10 Alcorn Avenue,
Toronto, Ontario, Canada M4V 3B2
Penguin Books (N.Z.) Ltd, 182–190 Wairau Road,
Auckland 10, New Zealand

Penguin Books Ltd, Registered Offices:
Harmondsworth, Middlesex, England

First published by Plume, a member of Penguin Putnam Inc.

First Printing, April 2002
10 9 8 7 6 5 4 3 2 1

LIBRARY OF CONGRESS CATALOGING-IN-PUBLICATION DATA:
Barefoot, Coy.
Thomas Jefferson on leadership : executive lessons from his life and letters / Coy Barefoot.
p. cm.
Includes bibliographical references and index.
ISBN 0-452-28311-6
1. Jefferson, Thomas, 1743–1826. 2. Jefferson, Thomas, 1743–1826—Quotations. 3. Presidents—United States—Biography. 4. United States—Politics and government—1775–1783. 5. United States—Politics and government—1783–1865. 6. Leadership—United States—Case studies. 7. Management—United States—Case studies. I. Title.
E332. B28 2002
973.4'6'092—dc21

2001058764

Printed in the United States of America
Set in New Baskerville
Designed by BTDNYC

For my Dad,
with love and thanks

CONTENTS

THE FIRST LESSON

Thomas Jefferson wasn't exactly what you might call a born leader. He was terribly shy and wary of crowds. He was not particularly attractive; he was gangly and given to slouching. In school he had a reputation for preferring his books to a night on the town. He wasn't especially charismatic. He disliked public speaking, and it showed. He was much too sensitive, and he often paid for it. He could be moody and emotional. He could be almost paranoid at times. He was often struck with self-doubt. He liked to be a homebody, and a lot of the time he just wanted to be left alone.

Yet Jefferson was undeniably one of the greatest leaders the world has ever known. Author of the Declaration of Independence, third president of the United States, secretary of state, ambassador to France, and founder of the University of Virginia, Jefferson's extraordinary life and accomplishments inspire men and women around the world to this day. A skilled statesman, philosopher, lawyer, scientist, musician, architect, writer, and farmer—Thomas Jefferson was among the brightest and most learned men of his generation. His leadership was, and continues to be, critical to the success of this great experiment in democracy we call the United States.

This shy, temperamental, bookish man overcame his personal limitations to become one of the most exemplary and influential leaders in world history. There is a great deal that each of us can learn from his example.

For most people, leadership is an acquired skill. Everyday men and women with enormous personal strikes against them have dared themselves to take on the challenge of leadership and have often succeeded beyond all expectations and have inspired others by their example. Some individuals do seem to be born with natural leadership abilities—people are drawn to them; they have a talent for inspiring us; they exude confidence; they instinctively know how to make things happen. But the rest of us have to study and practice leadership skills before we attain the status of a leader. Acquiring those skills means dedicating ourselves to greatness in our families, in school, in our chosen fields of endeavor, in our communities, and even as a nation.

Like most people, Jefferson was not a born leader, but throughout his life he was certainly willing to learn. He challenged himself at every turn, committed himself to gaining the knowledge and skills that he believed would make him a better human being and in turn inspire others to do so as well. That's ultimately what the American Enlightenment was all about: opening the mind to new ideas and challenges, and making a sincere effort to improve the lot of humankind. Learning to be a leader was an integral part of that formula.

That is the first lesson of Jefferson's exemplary life: Leadership is not limited to those few who come by it naturally. *Leadership can be learned.*

FINDING YOUR WAY

Surveying was a vocation in the Jefferson family for generations. By the time Tom Jefferson was born in the spring of 1743 in a farmhouse on the Virginia frontier, the family could boast a line of successful surveyors and explorers. Tom's father, Peter, was even something of a surveying celebrity, having co-written around 1750 one of the earliest and most complete maps of the colony.

For the English settlers traveling the colonial back country, mapping could be a dangerous job. Peter would regale Tom and his siblings with dramatic stories of his adventures—surviving attacks by wild animals, sleeping in trees, trudging hundreds of miles through the mountains, going without food or water, and eating raw animal flesh to stay alive. But with the right tools, some know-how, and genuine courage, Peter Jefferson and other surveyors of the period managed to navigate their way through what was, to them at least, uncharted and unpredictable wilderness.

As a boy Tom learned from his father the basics of surveying land and drawing and reading maps. These practical skills served him well his entire life, and they provided a foundation for the acclaimed architectural work he later pursued. Peter taught his son how to think clearly, get his bearings, and find his way. Most important, he taught him that the countryside around him could be captured in a well-calculated sketch. From his father's maps, young Tom learned how to use his mind to lift himself out of his immediate surroundings and to imagine the landscape from above: to see how the Rivanna River meandered south into the James, to picture the mountains around him reaching southwest toward the magnificent Blue Ridge, to see a carpet of green forests dotted with open fields and farms weave across the rolling Virginia Piedmont toward the ocean.

In this way, Peter Jefferson gave his son an exceptional gift. Thomas Jefferson learned how to see the larger landscape and to find his place in it. At an early age he became keenly aware that the natural world, which might at first appear limitless and incomprehensible to a child, was in fact entirely measurable.

With some concentration and skills, he could get his mind around it. He learned that reason and common sense were the keys to understanding where he was and how he was going to get where he needed to go.

Peter Jefferson did more than teach his son how to survey land and read maps—he prepared his mind for a lifetime of discovery. Thomas Jefferson believed that given the right information and tools, we can find a path through whatever wilderness lies before us. Disorder and the unknown are just temporary challenges we can overcome with a plan of persistence and investigation. His distinguished career was a testament to this important lesson he learned early in life.

Leadership necessitates forging a path: It requires us to accept challenges, to dare to make a difference, to discover order and balance. We must overcome limitations and fears. We must learn and teach.

Each one of us stands before an uncharted wilderness in our own lives, facing powerful dilemmas: what to do, where to go, how to get there, what step to take first. Before us great mountains rise, seemingly impassable. Wild rivers roar downstream where whitewater crashes on foreboding rocks. The forests are dark and full of wild beasts. Obstacles abound and challenges appear overwhelming.

But, we can find a way through. We can discover a path. We can get where we want to go. Getting there requires leadership. It demands courage and persistence. And we can learn the skills we need to find our way no matter what personal strikes we may have against us.

You may share many of the reservations that Jefferson himself had. You may be shy; you may not be a good public speaker; you may believe you're simply not worthy of the responsibility of leadership. That's okay. You're in good company. *Thomas Jef-*

ferson on Leadership is a map to help you navigate the landscape of Jeffersonian leadership. The lessons are all here, waiting to be put to use in your own life. What you do with them will be up to you. The challenge is yours. Your journey awaits.

> **"Truth advances and error recedes step by step only; and to do our fellow-men the most good in our power, we must lead where we can, follow where we cannot, and still go with them, watching always the favorable moment for helping them to another step."**
>
> **—THOMAS JEFFERSON,** ***1814***

THOMAS JEFFERSON ON LEADERSHIP

CHAPTER 1

JEFFERSON THE STUDENT

I was often thrown into the society of horseracers, cardplayers, foxhunters, scientific and professional men, and of dignified men; and many a time have I asked myself, in the enthusiastic moment of the death of a fox, the victory of a favorite horse, the issue of a question eloquently argued at the bar or in the great Council of the nation, well, which of these kinds of reputation should I prefer? That of a horse jockey? A foxhunter? An orator? Or the honest advocate of my country's rights?

Peter Jefferson passed away in the humid Virginia summer of 1757. He was fifty years old. Thomas Jefferson was just fourteen at the time, and he understandably took his father's death very hard. Peter left a wife, two sons, and six daughters. They lived on the family's tobacco plantation, Shadwell, along the Rivanna River, near what is now the city of Charlottesville.

During his final days Peter made it clear that the education of his eldest son was of utmost concern. He left instructions that Thomas was to receive the best classical schooling possible. Decades later, as an elderly man, Thomas Jefferson commented on his father's dying gesture. "Among the values of classical learning, I estimate the luxury of reading the Greek and Roman authors in all the beauties of their originals," he wrote in 1819. "I think myself more indebted to my father for this than for all the other luxuries his cares and affections have placed within my reach."

Like the children of other well-to-do planters in Virginia, Thomas Jefferson's education was a privileged and exclusive affair. In those years long before public schools were established, an education was almost always reserved for the sons (and some daughters) of affluent gentry, who could afford private tutors. Instruction was customarily offered by learned members of the clergy in their homes or in one-room schoolhouses.

Jefferson embarked on his schooling at age five. Beginning at the age of nine he spent five years studying Latin with the Reverend William Douglas. Shortly after Jefferson's father died, he entered the tutelage of Reverend James Maury. Maury's school was a humble building made of logs in the mountains near his home. The curriculum was founded on a thorough reading of Latin and Greek. There Jefferson immersed himself in the great works of the classical writers—including the histories of Herodotus, Thucydides, Livy, Caesar, and Tacitus, the poetry of Virgil, Homer, Euripides, and Sophocles, and the philosophy of Plato, Socrates, Cicero, and Seneca. He became thoroughly familiar with the trials and tribulations of Athenian democracy and of the Roman republic—lessons that proved to have a profound impact on his political thinking and that helped shape his vision for America.

SEIZE RESPONSIBILITY

Though he enjoyed this impressive education—a rare opportunity for a boy in rural Virginia in the 1750s—the lanky teenager continued to miss his father; the void was made all the worse by the fact that he was never all that close to his mother. Preeminent Jefferson biographer Dumas Malone has written that Peter's death "created a chasm" in young Tom's life. At such a formative age, when a boy is fast becoming a man, a son naturally looks to his father for guidance and support. But in a profound way, Tom Jefferson was on his own. He would later write,

> When I recollect that at 14 years of age the whole care and direction of myself was thrown on myself entirely, without a relation or friend qualified to advise or guide me, and recollect the various sorts of bad company with which I associated from time to time, I am astonished I did not turn off with some of them, and become as worthless to society as they were.

He may have been overstating the case to a degree, but the point is well taken. While still a boy, Thomas Jefferson was forced to take his first step on the road to leadership: assuming responsibility for himself. Before we can ever hope to lead others, to inspire them with our examples and achievements, we must begin by learning to lead ourselves.

We start by accepting responsibility for our actions, our characters, and our own paths in life—and not just accepting it, but embracing it, *seizing* it—recognizing the formidable power that responsibility offers us. Don't simply *assume* responsibility for yourself; it is much too potent a force to accept passively. Instead, grab it, snatch it up, own it, make it yours.

Thomas Jefferson once described responsibility as "a tremendous engine" at the very heart of a free society. Harnessing that power in your life means having the ability to no longer allow your circumstances to rule you. Seizing responsibility gives you the strength to set your own course. It empowers you with the capability to accept obligations and challenges head-on, then to reap the rewards that your successes inevitably offer.

As a young classical scholar, Jefferson would have known that at the root of the word "responsibility" is the Latin verb *respondere,* which means to pledge back or to make a solemn promise. Seizing responsibility in our lives is an act of honor: a promise we make, first to ourselves, that the buck stops right here and that no matter what happens in the adventure that is our life, we will always remain faithful to ourselves.

Responsibility poses a daunting task for any of us, let alone a teenage boy. It was a challenge that fate had thrust upon him, and young Tom rose to the occasion. It is fitting that the first example of Jefferson's writing that has survived illustrates this issue of seizing responsibility. In the winter of 1760, when he was just sixteen years old, Jefferson wrote a letter to the executor of his father's estate, explaining why he had decided to leave home and continue his education at the College of William and Mary. The style of the letter, in which he lays out his thinking on the matter, hints at the talented lawyer that he would soon become.

> In the first place, as long as I stay at the Mountains the Loss of one fourth of my Time is inevitable, by Company's coming here and detaining me from School. And likewise, my absence will in a great Measure put a stop to so much Company, and by that Means lessen the Expences of the Estate in House-Keeping. And on the other Hand by going to the College I shall get a more universal Acquaintance, which may hereafter be serviceable to me; & suppose I can pursue my Studies in the Greek & Latin as well there as here, and likewise learn something of the Mathematics.

Jefferson recognized the inherent values of leaving home and going off to school on his own. He knew that William and Mary would offer him lessons he could not possibly get in a one-room schoolhouse in the country—important lessons that would only come from meeting new people. He instinctively understood that knowledge and experience are equally important in life.

Like all great leaders who have achieved any measure of success, Jefferson learned at a relatively young age that life need not be something that just happens to us. Seizing responsibility for yourself, intelligently considering the options before you, and then charting your own course are the first brave steps on the road to leadership.

COUNTRY BOY COMES TO THE BIG CITY

Jefferson arrived in Williamsburg in the spring of 1760, just a few weeks shy of his seventeenth birthday. Then the epicenter of political and cultural life in the Virginia colony, Williamsburg was a bustling metropolis of about two thousand people. Duke of Gloucester Street teemed with lively taverns and busy shops. Ships from Europe and Africa regularly docked at nearby Jamestown. To a country boy from the mountains, Williamsburg must have seemed exotic, exciting, and overwhelming.

Jefferson matriculated at the College of William and Mary on March 25. He was among approximately one hundred students then under the guidance of less than half a dozen faculty members, all male and nearly all members of the clergy. Founded in 1683 and named for the Dutch King William III and Queen Mary II of England, the college enjoyed a solid reputation for its classical education of Latin, Greek, mathematics, and philosophy. Like most of his classmates, Thomas Jefferson boarded in the stately Sir Christopher Wren building.

Contemporary sources describe young Jefferson as gangling, red-haired, and freckled. Neither his looks nor his personality were considered to be particularly inspiring. Likely hoping to keep up with his new circle of well-to-do friends, Jefferson spent a great deal of money buying new clothes and renting horses and carriages. He wanted to look good, and he wanted people to like him. But in keeping with the commitment of responsibility that he had accepted, he sent the executor of his father's estate a complete list of his expenditures and "proposed that the amount of his expenses should be deducted from his portion of the property."

"No, no," his guardian kindly responded. "If you have sowed your wild oats in this manner, Tom, the estate can well afford to pay your expenses."

CULTIVATE THE HABIT OF INDUSTRY

Once he had had a chance to get settled in Williamsburg, Jefferson quickly buckled down and focused on his schoolwork. He began to develop what he would later call the "habit of industry," which meant making the most of his time both in and out of the classroom. He later described the approach in a letter to his daughter:

> Of all the cankers of human happiness none corrodes with so silent, yet so baneful an influence, as indolence. Body and mind both unemployed, our being becomes a burthen, and every object about us loathsome, even the dearest. Idleness begets ennui, ennui the hypochondriac, and that a diseased body. Exercise and application produce order in our affairs, health of body and cheerfulness of mind, and these make us precious to our friends. It is while we are young that the habit of industry is formed. If not then, then it never is afterwards. The fortune of our lives, therefore, depends on employing well the short period of youth. If at any moment, my dear, you catch yourself in idleness, start from it as you would from the precipice of a gulf.

One of the first tasks of responsible leaders is to focus their efforts on self-improvement. Thomas Jefferson's approach was to pursue a "habit of industry" by daily exercise of both mind and body.

THE MIND

The degree to which Jefferson valued the pursuit of knowledge cannot be overstated. Education was for him the key not only to personal happiness but also to a free and just society. The quest for "science"—as he usually called knowledge in general—was thus a noble and virtuous act that demanded a responsible commitment to self-improvement.

He wrote later in life, "If a nation expects to be ignorant and free in a state of civilization, it expects what never was and never will be." Freedom begins then with the mind, and the extent to which we are free and happy is largely measured by the commitment we are willing to give to learning new things and making ourselves aware of what's going on in the world around us.

Always an earnest student, Jefferson passionately threw himself into his studies at William and Mary. Though he took time out to attend parties, to visit the theater, to practice his violin, and to go dancing in the spacious Apollo Room at the Raleigh Tavern, his priorities were clear. He was at school to learn. A classmate later recalled that young Tom "could tear himself away from his dearest friends to fly to his studies."

Jefferson was mystified by how much time his fellow students wasted on horse racing, card playing, and drinking. William and Mary students certainly didn't have to go far to find a party in Williamsburg, and prostitution and gambling were common. To Jefferson, Williamsburg was a city of endless temptations; he even later referred to it several times as "Devilsburg." He was aware that his success often meant choosing his books over a night on the town. He displayed the talents of a true, self-disciplined leader by not allowing temporary distractions to steer him from his path.

He later shared this advice with his grandson, then studying in Pennsylvania. Reflecting the old adage that we often become like the people we spend time with, Jefferson wrote, "Look steadily to the pursuits which have carried you to Philadelphia, be very select in the society you attach yourself to; avoid taverns, drinkers, smokers, and idlers and dissipated persons generally; for it is with such that broils and contentions arise, and you will find your path more easy and tranquil."

THE BODY

No less important than improving the mind was exercising the body. Thomas Jefferson was a lifelong proponent of a rigorous regimen of daily fitness. "You are not," he once wrote his daughter, "to consider yourself as unemployed while taking exercise. That is necessary for your health, and health is the first of all objects."

Peter Jefferson had seen to it that his son knew well how to ride horses, to swim, and to hunt. As a boy Tom had enjoyed exploring the hills and fields near his home. There he developed what one biographer calls "that love of walking which never afterwards deserted him." In Williamsburg he even enjoyed jogging on the outskirts of the college, an activity pursued by William and Mary students to this very day.

Jefferson recommended devoting two hours each day to exercise, for "exercise and recreation are as necessary as reading; I will say rather more necessary, because health is worth more than learning. A strong body makes the mind strong." In a memorable letter to his grandson, Jefferson laid out his prescription for physical fitness:

> Walking is the best possible exercise. Habituate yourself to walk very far. There is no habit you will value so much as that of walking far without fatigue. I would advise you to take your exercise in the afternoon: not because it is the best time for exercise, for certainly it is not; but because it is the best time to spare from your studies; and habit will soon reconcile it to health, and render it nearly as useful as if you gave to that the more precious hours of the day. A little walk of half an hour, in the morning, when you first rise, is advisable also. . . . Rise at a fixed and an early hour, and go to bed at a fixed and early hour also. Sitting up late at night is injurious to the health, and not useful to the mind.

Jefferson was a fervent believer in making a daily habit of actions that reward us with wisdom, health, and happiness. To that end, seek to cultivate a habit of industry in your own life. Establish a plan that will prepare your mind and your body for the challenges that every leader inevitably encounters.

Following Jefferson's dictum for cultivating the "habit of industry" in our lives means developing a plan to balance our activities as well as challenge our minds and our bodies on a regular basis. It also means establishing and committing to priorities, and steadfastly refusing to allow the temptations of the day to distract us from work we know needs to be done. Jefferson once quipped, "It is wonderful how much may be done if we are always doing."

"MY GREAT GOOD FORTUNE"

While a student at the College of William and Mary, Jefferson took classes in mathematics, philosophy, and ethics from Dr. William Small, a recent emigrant from Scotland. Small had the distinction of being the only teacher on the faculty at the time who was not a member of the clergy, and Jefferson appreciated the absence of Christian dogma in his classroom.

It was in Dr. Small that young Jefferson found a kindred spirit. They were united in their feelings about religion as well as in their love for learning. Their friendship had a long-lasting effect on Jefferson's life.

"It was my great good fortune," Jefferson later wrote, "and what probably fixed the destinies of my life, that Dr. William Small of Scotland was then professor of mathematics, a man profound in most of the useful branches of science, with a happy talent of communication, correct and gentlemanly manners, and an enlarged and liberal mind. He, most happily for me, became soon attached to me and made me his daily companion when not engaged in the school, and from his conversation I got my first views of the expansion of science and of the system of things in which we are placed."

Later described as a torchbearer of the Enlightenment, Small introduced Jefferson to the works of Sir Isaac Newton and John Locke, and "opened before his eyes the vistas of an ordered universe." Jefferson biographer Dumas Malone has written that Small was "one of those rare men who point the way, who show new paths, who open doors before the mind."

Small was an eminently gifted teacher whose talents found a receptive and ardent pupil in Thomas Jefferson. Without realizing it, Small introduced the principles of the Enlightenment to a young man who would become one of their most enthusiastic advocates. At the core of Small's lessons was the conviction that knowledge could redeem humankind from the centuries-old chains of ignorance to which it had been sentenced; even more important, blind allegiance to authority was no virtue. Small helped put Jefferson on the path to seeing that the leaders of the future were not the priests or the kings who had ruled with an iron fist for so long, but rather the scientists, the educators, the artists, the philosophers, and those humanitarians who spoke out for the natural rights of life and liberty.

We can imagine Jefferson reading Newton, Locke, or the philosopher Francis Bacon late at night by candlelight, in his room in the Wren building or under the shade of an elm tree in the college yard, completely enthralled in discovery. It was an exciting time for him—and in retrospect a decisive moment in American history—as this young scholar first came in contact with the philosophical principles of freedom that would later find fruition in a new government.

A TRIUMVIRATE OF MENTORS

William Small not only opened "doors before the mind" of his favorite student, but also literally opened doors for him in Williamsburg. Accompanying Small, Jefferson soon found himself as a guest at the table of colonial governor Francis Fauquier, the most powerful man in Virginia. They were often joined by Small's close friend George Wythe, the professor of law at the college and one of the most notable attorneys in the colony.

Jefferson spent many enjoyable evenings listening to these three men discuss everything from science and philosophy to politics and art. He would afterwards fondly remember these dinners as some of the most gratifying episodes of his life. How fortunate he was, still just a college student, to be included in these affairs with three of the most learned men in Virginia—

all leaders in their own fields. Each in his way proved to be an invaluable mentor to Jefferson. It was here at Fauquier's table that Jefferson "heard more good sense, more rational and philosophical conversations than in all my life besides."

Thanks to the examples set by these men—who were to him the very models of successful leadership—he began to appreciate the inestimable value of character, integrity, and what he called "manners." He experienced firsthand genteel behavior, politeness, and civility as a guest at the governor's table. He admired the graciousness and the hospitality of Fauquier that made such pleasant evenings possible. It was an example he later sought to emulate, both as host at his home, Monticello, and as president in the White House.

Along with his mother's cousin, Virginia legislator Peyton Randolph, Jefferson found in this triumvirate of mentors compelling standards of virtue and leadership against which he could measure himself. He very consciously embarked on a quest to follow their lead. And he remained forever grateful that they showed such patience and kindness to a young student.

When in Williamsburg, he later recalled, "I had the good fortune to become acquainted very early with some characters of very high standing, and to feel the incessant wish that I could even become what they were. Under temptations and difficulties, I could ask myself what would Dr. Small, Mr. Wythe, Peyton Randolph do in this situation?"

Thomas Jefferson later hailed Williamsburg as "the finest school of manners and morals that ever existed in America." That's a far cry from calling it "Devilsburg," but the considerable experiences he had as a dinner guest in the Governor's Palace were a world away from the boozing and gambling he had witnessed among his classmates.

Like most leaders Jefferson benefited from the wisdom and generosity of capable mentors. He wisely apprenticed himself to these master craftsmen of great leadership. Displaying remarkable maturity while still a teenager, he learned to trust in the examples set by men he admired rather than always relying on what he called "the jaundiced eye of youth." It was a course of action that would serve him extremely well.

YOUR PERSONAL LEGACY

As a young man Jefferson prepared himself for leadership by accepting responsibility, developing a self-disciplined habit of industry, and by patterning himself after his mentors. But in another important way Jefferson revealed a quality that all great leaders share: a candid awareness of his own legacy.

As a student Jefferson was witness to the boisterous taverns on Duke of Gloucester Street as well as the refined dinners in the Governor's Palace. He was as familiar with the late-night gambling and bawdiness of some of his classmates as he was with the philosophical musings of Dr. Small and the erudite comments of Mr. Wythe.

"From the circumstances of my position," he later wrote, "I was often thrown into the society of horseracers, cardplayers, foxhunters, scientific and professional men, and of dignified men; and many a time have I asked myself, in the enthusiastic moment of the death of a fox, the victory of a favorite horse, the issue of a question eloquently argued at the bar or in the great Council of the nation, well, which of these kinds of reputation should I prefer? That of a horse jockey? A foxhunter? An orator? Or the honest advocate of my country's rights?"

Not everyone is willing to make a frank assessment of their own reputation. But it's a trait common among successful leaders. A reputation can be a powerful tool, one that can work for you or against you. Leadership means being mindful of your legacy—not obsessed with it, for that would allow ego to lord over virtue. Rather, like Jefferson, simply stop and ask yourself which reputation do you prefer? Consider the advice he once gave his grandson:

> When your mind shall be well improved with science, nothing will be necessary to place you in the highest points of view, but to pursue the interests of your country, the interests of your friends, and your own interests also, with the purest integrity, the most chaste honor. The defect of these virtues can never be made up by all the other acquirements of body and mind. Make these then your first object. Give up money, give up fame, give up science, give the earth itself and all it contains, rather than do an immoral act. And never suppose, that in any possible situation, or under any circumstances, it is best for you to do a dishonorable thing, however slightly so it may appear to you. Whenever you are to do a thing, though it can never be known but to yourself, ask yourself how you would act were all the world looking at you, and act accordingly. Encourage all your virtuous dispositions, and exercise them whenever an opportunity arises.

What's your own personal legacy? Granted, most of us don't have the media evaluating our every move or historians scrutinizing our decisions. But your spouse and your children watch you; your coworkers; your parents, your students, your friends, your employees, your neighbors. At some point, someone whose opinion matters greatly to you will be paying a lot of attention to your actions. They'll be watching what you do and how you react. You may not even be aware of it, but they will be looking for you to set an example because they need an example to follow. They'll be looking for a leader.

Each time you enter a room, attend a practice or a meeting—in fact, every time you involve yourself in the life of another human being—you have an opportunity to leave a positive token of your own legacy behind.

Take some quiet time by yourself and really give some thought to what you'd like your reputation to be. What do you want people to say about you when you're not around? What do you stand for? Do your actions demonstrate your beliefs? Are you exercising your "virtuous dispositions," or are they in need of a good workout?

A YOUNG LAWYER IN THE MAKING

In 1762, after two years of work at William and Mary, Jefferson embarked on his legal education. He was nineteen. He spent the next five years reading and studying the law in Williamsburg under the direction of George Wythe. At the time aspiring lawyers more commonly spent only a couple of years preparing for the bar. But Jefferson's tutelage under Wythe was anything but common. For one, they enjoyed a tremendously positive friendship. Wythe astutely recognized great potential and remarkable intelligence in the young man. And Jefferson looked up to the thirty-five-year-old attorney as a second father. "No man ever left behind him a character more venerated than George Wythe," Jefferson once wrote. "His virtue was of the purest tint; his integrity inflexible, and his justice exact. . . . Mr.

Wythe continued to be my faithful and beloved mentor in youth and my most affectionate friend through life."

There was much about Wythe that Jefferson admired and strove to emulate. He esteemed the man's passion for knowledge and lauded his personal sense of decorum. Jefferson later eulogized Wythe:

> Temperance and regularity in all his habits gave him general good health, and his unaffected modesty and suavity of manners endeared him to everyone. He was of easy elocution, his language chaste, methodical in the arrangement of his matter, learned and logical in the use of it, and of great urbanity in debate; not quick of apprehension but, with a little time, profound in penetration and sound in conclusion. Such was George Wythe, the honor of his own and the model of future times.

Wythe believed that his students preparing for the bar should do much more than simply read law books and listen in on the court. Being an attorney, for Wythe, was not just about preparing briefs and arguing cases. It was about being a leader in the community, being someone others could trust, respect, and look up to. To that end, Wythe saw to it that his students were highly educated and well versed in a variety of subjects, not just the law.

Through five years of directed readings, Wythe encouraged Jefferson to continue his studies in classical and foreign languages, mathematics, literature, philosophy, ethics, and oratory. He heartily endorsed Jefferson's insatiable curiosity and was always ready to recommend another book for his eager student to devour. It was about this time that a young woman in Williamsburg observed that she "never knew any one to ask so many questions as Thomas Jefferson." In the end, there was perhaps no better match between teacher and pupil than that of George Wythe and Thomas Jefferson.

Though he invested more of his time preparing for the bar than most other law students at the time, Jefferson—and in hindsight, the country—was better for it. Time has shown that he was not just fortifying his mind to assume the role of an attorney, but he was strengthening his understanding and awareness of the human condition, equipping himself with a well-informed perspective that would help make him one of the most inspiring leaders of a new nation.

In the course of study or practice, we are typically focused on the immediate challenge that lies ahead: the next test, the next game, the next meeting, the next big event. But often our greatest challenges—when our preparation is needed most—come later, in situations we could not have foreseen. Exceptional leaders know this. And that is why they are willing to go to greater lengths to prepare themselves and those in their care for the unexpected trials that inevitably lie in wait.

"BOLD IN THE PURSUIT"

During the five years he studied under the guidance of George Wythe, Thomas Jefferson continued to write in his literary commonplace book. Here Jefferson excerpted passages from his readings that made an impression on him. "Commonplacing," as it was known, was a widespread practice among scholars at the time. This was just one of many such notebooks Jefferson kept throughout his life.

He filled the blank pages of this little journal with lines from a host of writers, poets, and playwrights. For example, Jefferson recorded Shakespeare's observation that "in struggling with Misfortunes Lies the true Proof of Virtue"; from Euripides he noted: "For how can you win a great cause by small efforts?"

A close reading of his commonplace book reveals a young man struggling to understand life, death, God, law, and love. Jefferson said he copied these passages into his journal "at a time of life when I was bold in the pursuit of knowledge, never fearing to follow truth and reason to whatever results they led, and bearding every authority which stood in their way." Some lines he found illuminating, others inspiring. But the physical act of copying them down helped to focus his own understanding of the world around him and his place in it.

CLARIFY YOUR BELIEFS AND FOCUS YOUR GOALS

Have you written in your commonplace book lately? Do you have a private journal where you can write down words that inspire and motivate you? Many people who have achieved a measure of success in life appreciate the value of documenting their experience in writing and keeping a record of their progress. Privately committing your thoughts to paper—whether it be your greatest hopes, motivational messages, or inspirational words that comfort and sustain you—will have a powerful effect on your life. Writing these things down and returning to read them on a regular basis helps to clarify your beliefs and focus your goals.

Try an experiment: Beginning this week, start writing in your own commonplace book. Whenever you come across a passage in a book or magazine or hear a lyric in a song that really speaks to you, jot it down. It doesn't have to look pretty; Thomas Jefferson's commonplace book wasn't, with things written here and there in a sometimes bewildering fashion. The important thing is that you take the time to write them down. Make it your goal to have a daily entry in your commonplace book—something positive or compelling or interesting from each day. It might be a stirring passage from a novel you're reading, an affectionate line from a letter you received, or a goal you'd like to realize in your future. Try that for just two weeks, fourteen days, and see if the experience doesn't add something good and self-affirming to your life. It certainly did for Jefferson. Here are a few lines of his to help you get started with your own commonplace book:

> I have sworn upon the altar of God, eternal hostility against every form of tyranny over the mind of man. (1800)

> In endeavors to improve our situation, we should never despair. (1817)

> Honesty is the first chapter in the book of wisdom. (1819)

A NEW WORLD

Jefferson was admitted to the bar of the General Court of Virginia in 1767. He was twenty-four years old. Having received his father's inheritance three years earlier, which included thousands of acres of beautiful land in central Virginia, he was also quite wealthy for a man of his age.

Leaving home to study in Williamsburg had proven to be a rewarding and wise decision. He had taken advantage of a stellar education and had shown himself worthy of the friendship and kindness of his mentors. He had a bright future ahead of him. His formal years as a student were over, and a new world of opportunity and experience awaited him.

Jefferson the Student: Some Final Thoughts

During his years as a student Jefferson laid the groundwork for a life of leadership. It was a time for responsibility, a habit of industry, self-discipline, humility, and a quest for knowledge and experience. It was during this period that he learned and applied valuable lessons that served him well his entire life. Students can certainly contribute to their own success by paying heed to his example.

More broadly, you don't have to be a student officially enrolled in a school to benefit from Jefferson's model. There are numerous circumstances throughout our lives where we find ourselves in the role of a student—a new assignment, a new job, a new position on the team, any new challenge that forces us to recognize that we don't know everything we need to know to excel: a situation that compels us to study, learn new skills, and begin again before we can hope to lead.

Jefferson was a champion of self-improvement and education. He would have agreed that we should all retain the mindset of the student no matter how accomplished or successful we might become. Following his example, commit yourself to being a lifelong learner. School itself, he believed, should be only the beginning of a life of learning and study. In the last year of his life, Jefferson wrote: "We do not expect our schools to turn out their alumni already enthroned on the pinnacles of their respective sciences; but only so far advanced in each as to be able to pursue them by themselves . . . by energies and perseverances to be continued through life." Never relinquish the excitement of discovery in all your adventures.

- Before we can ever hope to lead others, to inspire them with our examples and our achievements, we must begin by learning to lead ourselves. Start by seizing responsibility for your actions, your character, and your own path in life.

- Cultivate the habit of industry by exercising both mind and body.
- Leaders are self-disciplined and focused on a plan of action. They are not easily distracted by the temptations of the day but are instead driven by the goals of tomorrow.
- "Be very select in the society you attach yourself to."
- Leaders recognize the inherent value in having a mentor, someone who has a proven track record of success. Emulate what you admire most about them; seek their counsel; and strive to learn all you can. When confronted with a dilemma, ask yourself how they might react.
- Leaders appreciate the power of a personal legacy. What do you want your reputation to be?
- Leaders are willing to take more time for practice and study in order to accomplish above-average things in their lives. Your greatest challenges lie ahead of you, waiting. So be prepared.
- Leaders know that curiosity is a good thing; they're not afraid to ask questions, and they encourage others to do the same.
- Have you written in *your* commonplace book lately? Writing things down will help clarify your beliefs and focus your goals.
- Truly inspiring leadership begins and ends with the mind of a student. Always be hungry for knowledge and skill.

CHAPTER 2

JEFFERSON THE ARCHITECT

Architecture is my delight, and putting up and pulling down one of my favorite amusements.

During the eventful years leading up to the Revolutionary War, 1767–76, Jefferson was engrossed in a multitude of tasks. He built a successful law practice, began designing and constructing his mountaintop home, Monticello, married and became a father, served in the Virginia House of Burgesses, and represented Virginia in the Continental Congress. It was during a meeting of congress in the summer of 1776 that he wrote the Declaration of Independence, the document for which he is most remembered.

TO THE MOUNTAIN

In the fall of 1769 Thomas Jefferson directed the first excavations on a rise just across the Rivanna River from Shadwell. The resulting hole in the red Virginia clay became the cellar of Monticello's South Pavilion, a one-room brick cottage eighteen feet square. Jefferson moved into this small outbuilding—his "bachelor's quarters" as he called it—in November 1770 as work on the main part of the house continued. This mountain would remain his home until his death nearly sixty years later.

He had chosen the site for his home years earlier. Jefferson's daughter recalled that "when quite a boy the top of this mountain was his favorite retreat, here he would bring his books to study, here would pass his holiday and leisure hours; that he never wearied of gazing on the sublime and beautiful scenery that spread around bounded only by the horizon, or the far off mountains; and that the indescribable delight he here enjoyed so attached him to this spot, that he determined when arrived at manhood he would here build his family mansion."

And family is just what he had in mind too when, just over a year later, on New Year's Day, 1772, he married Martha Wayles Skelton. She was a beautiful twenty-three-year-old widow five years younger than he. They had met while he was a student at William and Mary. They shared an affinity for literature, music, and were by every account very much in love. "In every scheme of happiness," he wrote, "she is placed in the fore-ground of the picture, as the principal figure. Take that away, and it is no picture for me." Over the next ten years they had six children, only two of whom, both girls, lived past childhood.

"MY DELIGHT"

The construction of what is now referred to as the first Monticello lasted until 1784. Jefferson later redesigned the house, nearly doubling its size with ever bolder additions from 1796 to 1809. The reconceptualizing of Monticello was a constant process of experimentation, design, and redesign that he thoroughly enjoyed. "Architecture is my delight," he wrote, "and putting up and pulling down one of my favorite amusements."

Eventually the mountaintop would be complemented by magnificent landscaping—trim lawns, colorful gardens, extensive orchards, and a vineyard. A series of carriage paths or "roundabouts" encircled the grounds, and a family cemetery was established in the shade of trees down the hill from the house.

The laborers and artisans who brought this vision to life were predominantly enslaved African Americans, many of whom Jefferson had inherited from his father and father-in-law. At one time Jefferson owned about 170 slaves on his various properties—roughly 70 of whom lived and labored on the mountain. Slavery was a contested and complex issue, and we will consider Jefferson's involvement with it in Chapter 6.

The study of architecture brought together in one pursuit many of his separate passions, particularly drawing, mathematics, and history. Always the mapmaker's son, he found use in the design of buildings and landscapes for the precision and logic of a surveyor combined with the creative force of an artist. Replete with clever innovations intertwined with classical motifs, Jefferson's home stands as one of the greatest achievements in American architecture. Monticello, he wrote, is my "poem in brick and mortar."

AN AMERICAN PALLADIO

The focal point of a five-thousand-acre estate, Monticello expressed the Roman neoclassical taste that Jefferson had come to love. A contemporary French visitor to Monticello commented that "we are safe to aver that Mr. Jefferson is the first American who has consulted the fine arts to know how he should shelter himself from the weather."

Far and away his greatest influence was the Italian Renaissance architect Andrea Palladio, who had achieved great success in the sixteenth century by incorporating the styles of Roman antiquity into his designs of Venetian country houses, or villas. Palladio found inspiring examples in the classical past, and his *Four Books of Architecture*, published in 1570, revolutionized architecture in the West.

Jefferson championed that revolution in the New World, seeing in Palladio's neoclassicism a certain elegance that the conservative architecture of colonial America was sorely lacking. He once even described the buildings in Williamsburg as "rude, misshapen piles" that resembled "brick kilns." Jefferson agreed with George Washington that architecture should "give symmetry, and just proportion to all the order and parts of the buildings, in order to please the eye."

Jefferson ardently led the vanguard to create an American architecture of neoclassical influence—an architecture that had, as he put it, a "ring of eternity." He described the challenge of reimagining American architecture in a 1785 letter to James Madison:

> How is a taste in this beautiful art to be formed in our countrymen, unless we avail ourselves of every occasion when public buildings are to be erected, of presenting to them models for their study and imitation? . . . You see, I am an enthusiast on the subject of the arts. But it is an enthusiasm of which I am not ashamed, as its object is to improve the taste of my countrymen, to increase their reputation, to reconcile them to the rest of the world, and procure them its praise.

With the goal in mind of teaching the public by example, Thomas Jefferson continued to refine his architectural skills by designing the Virginia State Capitol building in Richmond, his Poplar Forest country home in Bedford County, and many courthouses and private residences. He assisted Pierre L'Enfant in laying out the nation's new capital of Washington, and even created a design for the new capitol building and president's house (neither of which were built according to his plans, however).

THE DEFINING IDEAS

Jefferson's most inspiring masterwork as an architect was his design for the University of Virginia, which he founded in the last few years of his life. We will consider the university in more detail in a later chapter, but for now it's appropriate to point out that his architectural plans for the school—which he dubbed his "Academical Village"—expressed that same neoclassical sense of balance and order, mixed with a refreshing ingenuity.

Ten unique pavilions joined by student rooms, arcades, and colonnades form the east and west sides of a sublime courtyard, the glorious "Lawn." The stately Rotunda with its striking dome, based on the design of the Roman Pantheon, sits prominently at the north end. Encircled by brick serpentine walls, elegant gardens behind the pavilions organically link the Lawn to parallel ranges of dormitories and dining halls. Italian, Greek, French, and Chinese influences are manifest throughout the Academical Village. From Doric columns on Corinthian pedestals to far-eastern latticework in second-story railings, the University of Virginia is a visually breathtaking accomplishment.

It was for Jefferson the very model of an intellectual democratic community. It was an original American design literally written in the materials of the New World, red brick and wood. In 1976 the American Institute of Architects hailed Jefferson's Academical Village at the University of Virginia as the greatest architectural achievement in American history.

The outstanding potential of the Academical Village was realized in its designer's willingness to adapt the classical styles that so captivated him to a new place, a new time, and all-new circumstances. As University of Virginia architect Richard Guy Wilson has observed, Jefferson recast classical elements in American terms: "Classicism was the language of [his] literature, but it was elastic and was as capable of change and growth as knowledge."

In the very buildings he designed Jefferson thus illustrated his progressive vision for America. Not afraid to adapt and grow, willing to remake ourselves anew, we go forward with the best of the past as our guide and the best of the future as our goal. And as one historian has noted, Jefferson's "architecture still tugs at our sense of history. . . . His ideas continue to define what is 'American' in us: the need to reinvent and reconstruct for our own purposes, the desire for a distinctive national identity, and a quest for unity, driven by an inexplicable but powerful yearning for order, simplicity, and centrality."

Jefferson was attracted to Palladian architecture for much the same reason that he relished his study of the law with George Wythe. In both realms he discovered a coherent system of balance, order, logic, and precision that relied heavily on historical precedent. Neoclassical architecture, like the new laws he helped to write as a legislator, reflected the revolution in ideas that Jefferson found so enticing. It was a fascinating process of discovering timeless principles in a classical past and adapting them to the present day. Monticello, appropriately enough, has both an east and a west front—simultaneously looking back toward the past of an Old World and forward to a promising future in the New.

THE SIX P'S: LESSONS OF ARCHITECTURE

Exploring Jefferson's zeal for architecture reveals five salient qualities of his leadership formula: the combination of inspiration and personal inventiveness to realize potential; the ability to create an insightful plan for the future; the use of perspective in drafting those plans; the managerial skill of combining talented people with a plan of action; and the courage and perseverance to experiment, practice, and improve.

Past and Potential

No matter what course you have chosen, seek out inspiring examples of those who have gone before you. Palladio provided Jefferson with an appreciation for the enormous potential of architecture. But whether it's architecture or art, business or law, acting or athletics, there are men and women who have preceded you who offer exemplary accomplishments worthy of study. And that's just what we must do: Like Jefferson, we must meditate on our predecessor's work, learn their patterns, scrutinize their themes. In a nutshell, study their success; Jefferson made that a personal habit.

So moved, we are ready to take things to the next level and discover our true potential—where inspiration becomes leadership. Blend those examples that have taught and motivated you with your own personal style, your own flair, your own creativity. Build on the very best that has come before by combining it with *your* very best. That's what Jefferson did with Monticello and with his designs of the University of Virginia. He used his imagination to take Palladian architecture to a whole new level of beauty and form.

Ultimately, leaders aren't satisfied with the feeling of being inspired. That's not enough for them. They take an extra step. They work to give that feeling away. Let your inspiration inspire; allow your motivation to motivate; and use your knowledge to teach.

Plan

One of the most important elements of great leadership is the ability to create a plan for future action. Thomas Jefferson displayed this talent throughout his adult life. We see it in the innovative sketches of Monticello as well as in the timeless prose of the Declaration of Independence. We would expect as much from the son of a skilled mapmaker.

Good plans, like good maps, tell us where we are and where

we're headed, what we can expect, and how to prepare. They inform us where our goals lie and how we're going to reach them. They show us how elements will be arranged and how we fit into the big picture. And plans also help us to gauge our progress along the way.

Leaders don't let the course plot itself. They plan.

Perspective

Part of the nature of the work of an architect is to consider a subject from a variety of perspectives. Jefferson's plans for Monticello, for example, included a host of drawings—sketches of the building from above; bird's-eye views of the rooms; and elevated studies of the west and east fronts. There are detailed sketches of the staircases and columns, diagrams of how furniture could be laid out in the library, and even overhead diagrams showing how the building itself would fit into the landscape. Jefferson explored an enormous number of details at a variety of levels.

The best plans integrate the comprehensive perspective an architect brings to his or her work: considering subjects from a multitude of angles and views; studying minute details as well as the big picture; taking everything into account.

Perspective yields clarity to all the elements of a good plan.

People

A plan is only that and nothing more until it is put into action. Leaders are adept at bringing a solid plan together with talented individuals who know how to make things happen. A plan creates possibilities, but people make what's possible happen. To make his visionary home a reality, Jefferson enlisted the talents of George Dudley, a brick maker in Williamsburg, William Gates, an English stonemason, James Dinsmore, an Irish carpenter, John Hemings, an African-American joiner and carpenter, as well as an array of whites and free and enslaved blacks.

> **A truly inspired plan offers a way in which every individual can contribute to its success.**

Patience

Perhaps the greatest lesson we can draw from Jefferson's revolutionary architecture is that masterful achievement does not happen overnight. His first attempts at drawing a home for himself—a simple sketch with wavy lines—depicted a rather uninteresting wood building of just four rooms. It in no way resembled the monument to art and style that Monticello eventually became. But he stuck with it. Despite the fact that he was never professionally trained as an architect, he kept drawing, he kept imagining, and he kept studying.

He could easily have tossed that first drawing into the fire and simply hired an architect to build his house. But he had the perseverance, the courage, and ultimately the patience to experiment and to practice. Jefferson was infinitely comfortable with the learning process because he knew no matter what subject lay before him, he would only improve with time. And improve he did. Gradually, Jefferson acquired a superb talent for architecture. Those who have stood in Monticello's Entrance Hall or strolled on the University of Virginia's wide Lawn are intimately aware of just how profound that talent truly was.

Be patient. Give yourself the time you need to grow and improve.

Jefferson the Architect: Some Final Thoughts

Granted, few of us will ever design a building or create an original landscape. We can't all have the magical experience that the study of architecture offers. But in no small way, we are the architects of our own lives. The moment you seize responsibility for yourself, you become your own architect. Your future requires a solid foundation on which to build. Are you seeking inspiration from past examples? Are you studying the successes of those who've gone before you? Are you developing a plan with the right people in mind? Are you willing to muster the perseverance and patience that your endeavors require?

Your challenge is to build something beautiful, something magnificent—a unique life on your own terms, in your own style, that rewards you with happiness and accomplishment but also inspires others by your success. Each day offers you an opportunity to sketch new lines into your plans and integrate the influences that excite you. Don't toss your first efforts into the fire. Recognize them for what they are: merely the forerunners to your greatest achievements.

- Make it your personal habit to study the successes of those who have gone before. Your potential may be realized by integrating inspiring examples with your own creativity.
- Leaders aren't satisfied with the feeling of being inspired. They work to give that feeling to others.
- Good plans, like good maps, tell us where we are and where we're headed, what we can expect, and how to prepare. Lead by being the one who draws the plans.
- The best plans integrate the perspective of an architect, considering subjects from a multitude of angles. Take everything into account, from the most minute details to the big picture.
- A plan of action values unity and organization. It brings people together with a common cause and purpose in such a way that everyone has a way to contribute to its success.
- Leaders are not only adept at recognizing the talents of others but are proficient at putting those skills to work on a common goal.
- Get comfortable with the learning process. With patience and perseverance, you will only improve.
- You are the architect of your own life. Your challenge is to build something beautiful that inspires others.

CHAPTER 3

JEFFERSON THE REVOLUTIONARY

Kings are the servants, not the proprietors of the people. . . . The whole art of government consists in the art of being honest. Only aim to do your duty, and mankind will give you credit where you fail. . . . The God who gave us life gave us liberty at the same time; the hand of force may destroy, but cannot disjoin them.

These were years of great consequence for the American colonists. Though in hindsight it appears that a bloody war was inescapable, many Americans including Thomas Jefferson believed an armed conflict could be avoided, and they steadfastly labored to reconcile with England. Only when their efforts to peaceably secure their rights had been exhausted did they move to obtain them by force.

Throughout the difficult process, strong leadership was an essential ingredient to success. Then a bookish lawyer turned politician from the mountains of Virginia, Jefferson rose to national prominence in these years as one of those very leaders who offered the vision the fledgling nation so needed.

This chapter is titled "Jefferson the Revolutionary," for that is precisely the type of leader he became. But he didn't start out that way. He evolved over time from a freethinker to a rebel pledged to overthrowing a government. Expedited by his growing commitment to the principles of the Enlightenment, as well as his profound disappointment with and distrust of the English ruling class, his evolving vision was a process that took a few years to complete.

As we saw in the last chapter, Jefferson skillfully adopted elements of classical style—archways, domes, and columns—and combined them with his own ingenious vision to establish a fresh, uniquely American architecture. It was a new language in design. In much the same way he adapted elements of the Enlightenment—inalienable rights, freedom of mind, rule by an educated citizenry—to establish a uniquely American language of democracy. When it came to designing buildings Jefferson was as much a revolutionary as he was in laying out plans for a new republic. Jefferson demonstrated one of the fundamental facets of great leadership by finding resourceful ways to express timeless principles.

PAYING A "DEBT OF SERVICE"

Though many lawyers in Virginia at the time—certainly Patrick Henry was one—gained impressive reputations for their forceful oratory, Jefferson was not among them. In fact, throughout his life, he was never known as a convincing or moving public speaker. He never cared for it.

Dumas Malone has noted that "it was impossible for him to bellow; if he raised his voice it soon grew husky. No gathering that he attended in those years was ever very large, but even in a small, informal courtroom he could not hope to match Patrick Henry by appealing to the emotions of jurymen." One contemporary observer wrote that Jefferson displayed a "manner and voice femininely soft and gentle." At a time when a talent for oratory could be a surefire ticket to a position of leadership in the colony, Jefferson did not distinguish himself.

However, that did not prevent the voting citizens of Albemarle County (white males who owned at least twenty-five acres of land) from electing him their representative to the Virginia House of Burgesses in December 1768. Following in his father's footsteps—Peter Jefferson had once served in the House—Thomas Jefferson walked onto the stage of public life in May 1769. Thus in the same year that he began work on Monticello, the center of his private life, he entered public life for the first time.

As summer bloomed in the Tidewater, the twenty-six-year-old Jefferson took his seat in the Capitol building in Williamsburg where, only a few short years before, he had listened from the hallway with rapt attention as Patrick Henry spoke out vehemently against the Stamp Act. As he denounced the English parliament's right to tax the colonists, Henry had been assailed with shouts of "Treason!" by conservative loyalists. Henry had responded with intense resolve, "If this be treason then make the most of it." Jefferson never forgot that dramatic scene.

Jefferson considered his entry into public service a natural extension of the opportunities he had so far enjoyed. Neither an aggressive thirst for power nor a brazen quest for glory drove him into office; rather, he was motivated by a deep sense of responsibility, the honor of the position, and a modest but healthy dose of ambition. Jefferson once wrote to a friend that "there is a debt of service due from every man to his country." Having been so blessed to enjoy a first-rate education, a bountiful inheritance, and the friendship of some of the most progressive thinkers in the colony, Jefferson felt it his duty to step forward and lead.

LEADERSHIP IN THE FACE OF "NARROW LIMITS"

Interestingly, Thomas Jefferson's first term in public office lasted little more than a week. The royal governor, Botetourt, who had succeeded Francis Fauquier when he passed away, stepped in and summarily dissolved the House of Burgesses just ten days into their new term.

A year before, the legislators in Massachusetts had sought support among the colonies in their determined opposition to the Townshend Revenue Act—the infamous tax on tea, glass, paint, and paper that the English imposed on the colonists. Though they had been warned not to issue any resolutions in support of Massachusetts, the Virginia House of Burgesses did just that. In a unanimous vote on May 16, 1769, the burgesses resolved that only the colonial legislatures, not the parliament in London, had the right to tax the colonists.

Under directives from England, Botetourt had no choice then but to dissolve the assembly and call for a new election. The whole lot of Virginia representatives, including Thomas Jefferson, had effectively been fired for insubordination.

"The Governor dissolved us," he later recalled, "but we met the next day in the Apollo [Room] of the Raleigh Tavern." There the band of legislators resolved to stay committed to their cause. They remained largely loyal to the king, but maintained a stalwart opposition to parliament's policies. In a symbolic gesture, they agreed not to import or to buy taxed British goods.

Jefferson and most of the others were subsequently reelected to office in September. This would not be the last time, however, that the royal governor would dissolve the Virginia government. Nor would it be the last time the legislators would reconvene at the Raleigh Tavern to confirm their shared determination to persevere.

Recalling those tumultuous years in the House of Burgesses before the revolution, Jefferson wrote that "our minds were circumscribed within narrow limits by a habitual belief that it was our duty to be subordinate to the mother country in all matters of government, to direct all our labors in subservience to her interests, and even to observe a bigoted intolerance for all religions but hers."

In retrospect it is clear that the rebellion had already begun. It commenced, not with arms, but with words; not on the battlefield, but in the meeting house. The heated debates among colonial legislators in Virginia, Massachusetts, and elsewhere would eventually boil over into the streets of Williamsburg, Boston, and Philadelphia. Those "narrow limits" of "habitual belief" would give way to the force of progressive leaders committed to thinking differently and being courageous enough to stand on their convictions.

A "STATE OF INSENSIBILITY"

Confident in his leadership, the voters in Albemarle County regularly returned Jefferson to the House of Burgesses. He became quite familiar with the journey between Monticello and Williamsburg. And he paid close attention as the conflict between the Americans and British grew violent. On March 5, 1770, British soldiers in Boston fired on a crowd of men and boys who had been throwing snowballs at them. Five colonists were killed and six others wounded.

In the wake of the "Boston Massacre," things were relatively uneventful for a couple of years, as Jefferson himself observed with a touch of impatience: "Nothing of particular excitement occurring for a considerable time, our countrymen seemed to fall into a state of insensibility to our situation. The duty on tea, not yet repealed, and the Declaratory Act of a right in the British Parliament to bind us by their laws in all cases whatsoever still suspended over us." America, however, was soon to be shaken from that state of "insensibility."

In the summer of 1772 colonial rebels ran a British schooner, the *Gaspee*, aground on a sandbar off the coast of Rhode Island, looted and burned it, then captured its crew. The *Gaspee* and its commander, Royal Navy Lieutenant William Duddingston, were notorious for patrolling the waters off Rhode Island, ambushing ships, and seizing the cargo of colonial merchants—nothing but English despotism, the rebels argued. So to the Americans, Duddington certainly had it coming. It was payback time.

This was the first incident of a planned attack on the British military by American colonists. Parliament was incensed and attempted to have the perpetrators arrested and extradited to England to stand trial for treason. A yearlong investigation of this "Gaspee Affair" followed, but no one was charged with any crimes, as the identity of the rebels was kept a secret by everyone involved.

"FORWARDNESS AND ZEAL WHICH THE TIMES REQUIRED"

When the Virginia House of Burgesses convened early the next year, the *Gaspee* incident and subsequent investigation were on everyone's mind. But for Thomas Jefferson and some others, they were not high enough on the agenda. Apparently the older, more conservative legislators from elite Tidewater districts dragged their feet in responding to the Gaspee Affair. They were wary of worsening already strained relations with England—perhaps, as some have concluded, because it might be bad for trade.

To Jefferson, these men were overly politic and too cautious to take the bold stand that the situation demanded. Colonists in Rhode Island had stood up to the Royal Navy, then the most powerful military force on the planet. Though some observers tried to dismiss it as a minor act of terrorism, others viewed it as a hopeful sign that some Americans, at least, were willing to fight for better treatment from England.

Jefferson felt strongly that the episode demanded a swift and coordinated response from all the colonies. The time had come to speak with one voice. But there was no continental congress as yet, no representative assembly uniting the colonies, not even a standing committee for shared concerns. The colonies were like thirteen separate islands. It was clear that one of them would have to take the lead and coordinate some communication; Jefferson was disappointed when the more experienced members in the Virginia House of Burgesses failed to seize that opportunity. Not finding the kind of leadership they were seeking, Jefferson and some of the more radical legislators decided that the time had come for them to set their own example.

Recalling the aftermath of the *Gaspee* incident, Jefferson would later describe this critical moment: "Not thinking our old and leading members up to the point of forwardness and zeal which the times required, Mr. [Patrick] Henry, Richard Henry Lee, Francis L. Lee, Mr. [Dabney] Carr and myself agreed to meet in the evening in a private room of the Raleigh to consult on the state of things." It would prove to be a profoundly historic event.

On that Thursday night, March 4, 1773, Jefferson and the others formed Virginia's Committee of Correspondence with the aim of coordinating communication and action among the colonies. This would prove to be the beginning of a unified stand against English rule in America. Jefferson later wrote,

> We were all sensible that the most urgent of all measures was that of coming to an understanding with all the other colonies to consider the British claims as a common cause to all, and to produce a unity of action; and, for this purpose, that a committee of correspondence in each colony would be the best instrument for intercommunication and that their first measure would probably be to propose a meeting of deputies from every colony at some central place.

This revolutionary caucus therefore drew up its proposals and moved that Jefferson be the one to present them to the House of Burgesses. But in true form, Jefferson passed on the honor so as to encourage the prospects of others. "I argued that it should be done by Mr. Carr," he later wrote, "my friend and brother-in-law, then a new member, to whom I wished an opportunity should be given of making known to the house his great worth and talents. It was so agreed."

Just over a week later, on Friday, March 12, 1773, Dabney Carr rose in the House of Burgesses and proposed that Virginia take the lead by establishing the Committee of Correspondence to rally for a consensus of action among the colonies. After some debate, the proposal was accepted. "This Committee of Correspondence was unique," one historian has written, "in that it reached outside of the boundaries of Virginia in the hopes of tying together the colonies as one larger and more powerful group. This committee is the first hint of a united nation in America."

Faced with yet another rebellious assembly bent on stirring up trouble, Virginia's royal governor again dissolved the House of Burgesses and called for new elections. But the legislators, spurred on by Jefferson's defiant faction, left the Capitol and reconvened at the Raleigh Tavern; there they agreed to press on with their plans to establish a unified coalition of all the colonies.

"ALARM THEIR ATTENTION"

That same year there came a fateful quarrel over tea. In an effort to help the British East India Company avoid bankruptcy, Parliament decreed in 1773 that the company could unload its surplus tea in the American colonies without paying any import taxes—thereby undercutting the American merchants and effectively monopolizing the tea trade. Many colonists saw this as yet another gesture by the British elite that showed that America's interests were wholly unrepresented in Parliament.

Men and women throughout the colonies mobilized to boycott the cheap tea in protest. The action was particularly effective in that it brought conservative colonial merchants together with radical patriots—some worried about a monopoly that had been created with the help of the British government, others more concerned with the assault on colonial sovereignty.

On the night of December 16, 1773, a band of men poorly disguised as Mohawk Indians boarded a ship and dumped more than 340 crates of tea into Boston Harbor. As news of this "Boston Tea Party" spread, similar raids were made in ports up and down the coast. Parliament retaliated in the spring and summer of 1774 by passing the Coercive Acts—known in the colonies as the Intolerable Acts. Since Boston refused to pay for the destroyed tea, its colonial charter was revoked, its port was to be closed, and any unapproved public meetings of its legislators were declared illegal. The entire colony was to be shut down. To add insult to injury, Parliament ruled that colonists in Massachusetts must feed and house British troops on demand.

Then meeting in Williamsburg, the Virginia House of Burgesses reacted to the bad news coming out of Boston. Jefferson remembered that the Intolerable Acts "excited our sympathies" and motivated his caucus to action.

> The lead in the House on these subjects being no longer left to the old members, Mr. Henry, R.H. Lee, Fr. L. Lee, three or four other members whom I do not recollect, and myself, agreeing that we must boldly take an unequivocal stand in the line with Massachusetts, determined to meet and consult on the proper measures. . . . We were under conviction of the necessity of arousing our people from the lethargy into which they had fallen as to passing events, and thought that the appointment of a day of general fasting and prayer would be most likely to call up and alarm their attention.

June 1, the day the Boston port was to be closed, was chosen as a "day of fasting, humiliation, and prayer to implore Heaven to avert from us the evils of civil war, to inspire us with firmness in support of our rights, and to turn the hearts of the King and Parliament to moderation and justice." Jefferson noted that once June 1 was approved by the House without opposition, "the Governor dissolved us, as usual."

The assembly reconvened in the Apollo Room and there voted to organize a "Continental Congress" so that disagreements with England could be handled more effectively. It was hoped that such an assembly, with representatives from every colony, could bring America and England to a peaceful reconciliation before things got any worse. It was agreed that this new congress would meet in Philadelphia in September.

The June 1, 1774, day of prayer went on as scheduled. "The people met generally," Jefferson wrote, "with anxiety and alarm in their countenances, and the effect of the day through the whole colony was like a shock of electricity, arousing every man and placing him erect and solidly on his centre."

FACING CHALLENGES

How often have you found yourself up against "narrow limits" of "habitual belief"? What do you do when faced with a "state of insensibility" or "lethargy" in those you're aspiring to lead? Have you ever found your leaders too cautious and not "up to the point of forwardness and zeal which the times require"? At some time in our lives, it seems, we all face similar situations. There is much we can learn from how Jefferson reacted to these challenges. Here are five key principles of Jeffersonian leadership to keep in mind.

1. Question Authority

Begin by having the tenacity to question authority in all its forms. Such healthy skepticism is a useful tool of leadership and was integral to the tenets of the Enlightenment that Jefferson embraced. Moreover, it is at the heart of what it means to live freely. We are each called on to think for ourselves, to observe, to deduce, to learn, and to act with confidence in our beliefs.

The men and women who stood against the tyranny of the British rulers had the courage to question inherited authority. The colonists respected their own self-worth and potential, individually and as a nation. They questioned the legitimacy of those "narrow limits" of "habitual belief" that had been handed down to them as natural laws. They did what each one of us must do: They trusted their instincts.

Thomas Jefferson once wrote that "it behooves our citizens to be on their guard, to be firm in their principles, and full of confidence in themselves. We are able to preserve our self-government if we will but think so." Question authority with respect, humility, due diligence, and discretion; and listen closely when it answers. Only then can we hope to awaken from that slumber which Jefferson wrote about in 1807:

> It would seem impossible that an intelligent people with the faculty of reading and right of thinking should continue much longer to slumber under the pupilage of an interested aristocracy of priests and lawyers, persuading them to distrust themselves and to let them think for them. . . . Awaken them from this voluntary degradation of mind! Restore them to a due estimate of themselves and their fellow citizens, and a just abhorrence of the falsehoods and artifices which have seduced them!

Freedom itself relies on our willingness to think critically, ask questions, and believe in our potential. We demonstrate that belief each time we question the actions of any authority that wields influence over our lives.

2. *Rally Your Caucus*

Certainly one of the most effective steps Thomas Jefferson took as a junior member of the House of Burgesses was to coordinate his actions with like-minded representatives. He talked regularly with Patrick Henry, the Lees, and especially Dabney Carr about the business of the House. They openly shared their reactions and opinions with one another. They learned to work together as a tight core, committed to a common vision.

Here is where Jefferson, wary of public speaking, was at his best—as a contributor to a small group with whom he identified. He blossomed in committee. In a close circle of his compatriots, he felt comfortable to weigh in on the issues of the day. Successful leaders seek out those who share their beliefs and rally them into a committed nucleus for future action.

3. *Summon Boldness and Passion*

Plugged into a core group of fellow leaders who shared his views, Jefferson took that next decisive step when he joined them for a meeting at the Apollo Room in the Raleigh Tavern following the Gaspee Affair. Remember the very words he used: "Not thinking our old and leading members up to the point of forwardness and zeal which the times required . . . "

"Forwardness and zeal"—today we might more commonly use the words *boldness* and *passion*. Jefferson and his fellow revolutionaries searched for boldness and passion in the leaders of the Virginia House of Burgesses, and were disappointed when those traits didn't materialize. These leaders were too stuck in their ways and too afraid, for whatever reason, to rock the boat. To these men—whom, be assured, he greatly respected—Jefferson looked for a bold willingness to stand on principle, but he didn't find it. He wanted to see in them a passion for taking the lead in a cause he knew was just, but they failed to act. So Jefferson and his crew seized the moment and did what they thought should be done. It was just a matter of time before that older generation was following their lead.

It's a crossroads that every successful leader eventually comes to. What do you do when your leaders no longer express the boldness and passion that once inspired you? How should you react when they fail to take the higher ground? Should you throw in the towel and go home? Thomas Jefferson didn't. Patrick Henry didn't.

The lesson is clear: If you don't see effective leadership where and when you think it is needed most, then step in and become a leader yourself. Be the one to set the example that you've been looking for. The old saying is true: Leadership is seldom given; it is taken. And it is taken by those who are willing to manifest the boldness and passion that the times require.

4. Make an Emotional Appeal to the People

Jefferson was not the first leader challenged with overcoming "a state of insensibility" and "lethargy" in others. Apathy can be one of the most trying roadblocks a leader faces in summoning people to action. Jefferson found it particularly difficult to deal with, considering his belief that "the people . . . are the only sure reliance for the preservation of our liberty." He also wrote that it is "the people to whom all authority belongs." But what if the people have been lulled into believing that they have no power, as was the case for many in the colonies prior to 1776?

How should a leader respond if the people are insensible, lethargic, and apathetic? For Jefferson, lethargy among a nation's citizens was nothing less than "the forerunner of death to the public liberty."

In concert with his core group of revolutionaries in Williamsburg, Jefferson decided the ideal move was to call for a day of fasting and prayer. In other words, get everyone involved in an emotional way and on a personal level. Recall the words he used to explain the situation: "We were under conviction of the necessity of arousing our people from the lethargy into which they had fallen as to passing events, and thought that the appointment of a day of general fasting and prayer would be most likely to call up and alarm their attention."

The most expedient way to arouse others from apathy, following Jefferson's example, is to make an immediate, direct, and emotional appeal. Act expeditiously to arouse their sentiments, strike a chord with their feelings, hit them where they live, and "alarm their attention." Once you have others emotionally involved, you can present them with the logic and information at the crux of your plan. But you must get their attention first.

5. Coordinate a Unified Action

The Committee of Correspondence that Jefferson helped to found is now recognized as one of the first important steps the colonies took toward unifying as one nation. The stepped up communication among the thirteen colonies led to the formation of the Continental Congress, which brought them together as never before. It was this coordination that laid the foundation for a unified front and eventually a successful revolution. Without it, each colony was on its own—weak and vulnerable. Leaders strive to open up channels of communication that will bring individuals and organizations together to act as one. Unified action makes greater strength possible and offers a deeper sense of purpose.

A SUMMARY VIEW

In anticipation of the first meeting of the Continental Congress in the fall, Jefferson prepared a written draft of comments that he hoped the Virginia delegates would take with them to the meeting. He assumed the congress would make some kind of declaration to the king and was optimistic that his thoughts might be considered when it came time to write that document.

He later remembered, "I set out for Williamsburg some days before that appointed for our meeting, but was taken ill of a dysentery on the road and unable to proceed. I sent on therefore to Williamsburg two copies of my draft, the one under cover to Peyton Randolph, who I knew would be in the chair of the convention, the other to Patrick Henry. . . . It was read generally by the members, approved by many, but thought too bold for the present state of things; but they printed it in pamphlet form under the title of *A Summary View of the Rights of British America.*"

Jefferson's *Summary View,* as one historian has observed, was "blistering and revolutionary in content, robust and sweeping in style. . . . He was discreet in tone, yet the implication of revolution was unmistakable in his conclusion." In it Jefferson appealed directly to King George, boldly laying out the reasons why Parliament had no authority over the colonies:

> Kings are the servants, not the proprietors of the people. Open your breast, Sire, to liberal and expanded thought. Let not the name of George the Third be a blot on the page of history. . . . The whole art of government consists in the art of being honest. Only aim to do your duty, and mankind will

> give you credit where you fail. No longer persevere in sacrificing the rights of one part of the empire to the inordinate desires of another; but deal out to all equal and impartial right. . . . It is neither our wish nor our interest to separate from [Great Britain]. . . . Still less let it be proposed that our properties within our own territories shall be taxed or regulated by any power on earth but our own. The God who gave us life gave us liberty at the same time; the hand of force may destroy, but cannot disjoin them.

Jefferson later said that it was his goal in writing the *Summary View* to "set a pace that would bring the front and rear ranks of fellow countrymen together." Though his superiors in the House of Burgesses may have thought that pace was "too bold," many Americans thought it was right on target, and it did indeed bring people together.

Over the next few months, the twenty-three-page pamphlet was printed throughout the colonies. It even appeared in England where, Jefferson later learned, his name was added to the short list of dangerous rebels causing problems in America. Though at first he was not happy that his writings were being published and circulated without his knowledge—the pamphlet was, after all, treasonous—he later spoke of it with pride. "If it had any merit," he commented, "it was that of first taking our true ground, and that which was afterwards assumed and maintained."

The 1774 *Summary View of the Rights of British America* proved to be the beginning of Thomas Jefferson's far-reaching reputation as an exceptional writer who could eloquently express the ideals of natural rights and self-determination. Thereafter, the high estimation of his talent preceded him. The success of the *Summary View* became one of the principal reasons he was later asked to write the Declaration of Independence. Just thirty-one years old, Thomas Jefferson had entered a new phase in his development as a leader.

"AS FOR ME . . ."

The First Continental Congress met in Philadelphia on September 4, 1774. Peyton Randolph of Virginia was at the helm of the momentous gathering. Other luminaries in attendance included George Washington, Patrick Henry, and cousins Samuel and John Adams. Although an increasingly important leader, Jefferson was still a junior—and some thought overly zealous—member of the Virginia Assembly. Though he was not chosen to attend this first congress, he was selected as an alternate.

When they adjourned in late October 1774 the First Continental Congress had agreed to suspend all trade between England and the colonies, and to establish Committees of Safety to enforce the embargo. The colonists hoped that a peaceful economic blockade would compel Parliament to repeal the Intolerable Acts. The Congress also resolved to convene a Second Continental Congress the following May.

Jefferson did attend the Virginia Convention, however, which was held a few months later at St. John's Church in Richmond. A gathering of the burgesses without authorization from the royal governor, the revolutionary meeting took place in March 1775. Historian Wendell Garrett has written that "when the convention assembled it was clear that opinion was divided between conservatives who wanted to avoid a rupture with England at any cost and radical patriots who thought that military preparations should be undertaken at once."

Patrick Henry was one of those "radical patriots" who proposed that Virginia begin immediately to outfit an army. His landmark speech in support of the plan, given without notes and with his usual vigor, concluded:

> Gentlemen may cry, "Peace! Peace!"—but there is no peace. The war is actually begun! The next gale that sweeps from the north will bring to our ears the clash of resounding arms! Our brethren are already in the field! Why stand we here idle? What is it that gentlemen wish? What would they have? Is life so dear, or peace so sweet, as to be purchased at the price of chains and slavery? Forbid it, Almighty God! I know not what course others may take; but as for me, give me liberty, or give me death!

Though Jefferson's exact words are not known, it was noted that he argued heartily on the same side as Patrick Henry. The arguments of the younger patriots, led by Henry's moving words, rallied the conservative loyalists to action and the convention at last agreed to establish an army of Virginia.

LEXINGTON AND CONCORD

Only a few weeks later violence broke out in Massachusetts. Boston was under a military lockdown by the British, but colonial militias were forming in the small towns and countryside outside the city. In an effort to seize their weapons and arrest rebel leaders, British troops set out from Boston and descended on the small town of Lexington. There on the town green, on April 19, 1775, the British encountered a resistance of armed colonists under command of Captain John Parker. Historians are still not certain who fired the first shot, but a skirmish ensued that left some Americans dead.

The British moved on from there to Concord, where most of the colonial military supplies had already been hidden. Here the British soldiers encountered a much larger resistance and were forced to retreat to Boston. The colonial militia continued to fire on the British troops all the way back to the city. Nearly three hundred British soldiers and roughly one hundred Americans lay dead. By the time summer had rolled around, the colonial patriots had besieged Boston and surrounded the British troops there. The bloody war for liberty had begun.

"OUR CAUSE IS JUST"

When Peyton Randolph was called back to Virginia for an important meeting with the governor, Jefferson was sent to take his place at the Second Continental Congress in Philadelphia. He arrived there in a blistering hot June 1775. He was one of the youngest members present. John Adams later recalled:

> Mr. Jefferson came into Congress in June 1775, and brought with him a reputation for literature, science and happy talent of composition. . . . Though a silent member in Congress, he was so prompt, frank, explicit, and decisive upon committees and in conversation—not even Samuel Adams was more so—that he soon seized upon my heart.

Among its actions, the Second Continental Congress moved to equip a continental army and appointed George Washington as its chief officer. Because of his reputation as the author of the *Summary View,* Jefferson was chosen to serve on a committee charged with drafting a "Declaration of Causes for Taking Up Arms." Not surprisingly, some of the committee members thought the young Virginian's draft of this document was, as they put it, "too strong" and included too many "offensive statements."

So it was left to John Dickinson of Pennsylvania to prepare

the final, less radical version. In it, however, Dickinson included some excerpts from Jefferson's draft, which included the lines: "Our cause is just. Our union is perfect" and "Our attachment to no nation upon earth should supplant our attachment to liberty." The declaration was widely circulated and well-received by many colonists.

"FREE AND INDEPENDENT STATES"

Thomas Jefferson rejoined the Congress the following summer, 1776. He had recently endured the death of his mother, and before that, the sad passing of his baby daughter. He had begun to suffer from migraine headaches, which would plague him on and off for the rest of his life. Meanwhile, the colonies were ravaged with war.

On May 15, 1776, the Virginia Convention voted to instruct its delegates in Philadelphia to propose a resolution in Congress declaring the thirteen colonies "free and independent States." The proposed resolution was entered on June 7 by delegate Richard Henry Lee and followed by days of heated debate. Jefferson recalled that it was clear that some of the colonies "were not yet matured for falling from the parent stem, but that they were fast advancing to that state; it was thought most prudent to wait a while for them and to postpone the final decision to July 1."

In the meantime, another committee was selected to draft a "Declaration of Independence" that would accompany this resolution. The committee members, appointed on June 11, included John Adams, Benjamin Franklin, and Thomas Jefferson. Adams later remembered the committee's first meeting, at which he and Jefferson had a most memorable exchange:

> Jefferson proposed to me to make the draft. I said, 'I will not.' 'You should do it.' 'Oh! no.' 'Why will you not? You ought to

do it.' 'I will not.' 'Why?' 'Reasons enough.' 'What can be your reasons?' 'Reason first, you are a Virginian, and a Virginian ought to appear at the head of this business. Reason second, I am obnoxious, suspected, and unpopular. You are very much otherwise. Reason third, you can write ten times better than I can.' 'Well,' said Jefferson, 'if you are decided, I will do as well as I can.' 'Very well. When you have drawn it up, we will have a meeting.'

"AN EXPRESSION OF THE AMERICAN MIND"

Over the next couple of weeks Thomas Jefferson secluded himself in his rented, second-floor apartment in Philadelphia where he wrote the Declaration of Independence. He was thirty-three years old. He consulted "neither book nor pamphlet" but did integrate many of the revolutionary ideas of the Enlightenment that he had read about since his college days. He would later recall that in writing the declaration he had not tried to

> find out new principles, or new arguments never before thought of, nor merely to say things which had never been said before; but to place before mankind the common sense of the subject in terms so plain and firm as to command their assent, and to justify ourselves in the independent stand we are compelled to take. Neither aiming at originality of principle or sentiment, nor yet copied from any particular and previous writing, it was intended to be an expression of the American mind, and to give to that expression the proper tone and spirit called for by the occasion.

After some minor edits by Franklin and Adams, the declaration was submitted to Congress on Friday, June 28. The following week the delegates argued over the final form of the document and debated its merits. Benjamin Franklin noticed Jefferson "writhing a little under the acrimonious criticisms on some of its parts." But overall the Virginian remained silent and modestly allowed his draft to be edited. Some passages, including a condemnation of slavery, were completely deleted.

On June 2, Richard Henry Lee's original proposal that Congress declare the colonies free and independent states received nearly unanimous support. (The New York delegates abstained, then voted to support the resolution about two weeks later.) On July 4 the final wording of the Declaration of Independence was decided and the document approved. After it was officially printed later that month, most of the delegates signed the document on August 2. A new nation was born.

"THE SIGNAL"

> We hold these truths to be self-evident: that all men are created equal; that they are endowed by their Creator with certain inalienable rights; that among these are life, liberty, and the pursuit of happiness; that to secure these rights, governments are instituted among men, deriving their just powers from the consent of the governed; that whenever any form of government becomes destructive of these ends, it is the right of the people to alter or to abolish it and to institute new government, laying its foundation on such principles and organizing its powers in such form as to them shall seem most likely to effect their safety and happiness.

In its timeless and stirring prose, Thomas Jefferson's masterpiece continues to offer inspiration to people from all walks of life around the globe. "We hold these truths to be self-evident" has become an inspirational phrase for free nations everywhere. And the visionary declaration has emerged as a charter for what it means to be a free individual in a civil society. It set the United States on course to become a model of representative government for the entire world. Jefferson wrote that he hoped America's independence would be "the signal for arousing men to burst the chains under which monkish ignorance and superstition had persuaded them to bind themselves, and to assume the blessings and security of self-government."

The Declaration of Independence bid a resolute farewell to a world based on blind allegiance to a ruling class of aristocrats and instead advocated a world where people would be united in their support of common ideals. Paramount among these were the rights each one of us has to "life, liberty, and the pursuit of happiness." The Declaration was the achievement of which Jefferson was most proud, and for which he was most renowned.

With this single act Thomas Jefferson madc an indelible mark on the pages of history. He entered the pantheon of eminent leaders who have shaped the course of world civilization. In writing the Declaration of Independence, Jefferson displayed five additional principles that are fundamental to successful leadership.

1. Craft a Compelling Vision

Foremost among these principles was Jefferson's ability to craft a compelling vision. The Declaration of Independence is perhaps the most visionary document in American history, calling on each one of us to join in the pursuit of a free and just society. Just as he had done with his architectural designs, Jefferson integrated inspiring elements from his readings to create a new language of democracy.

He melded the Enlightenment principles of self-government, inalienable rights, and rule by an educated citizenry into a trumpet call for freedom that still resounds. Underlying this vision was the firm belief that people have an inherent right to oppose an institution that becomes destructive of their rights. In his declaration Jefferson laid out point by point exactly how the king and parliament had violated the natural rights of the colonists. The English ruling class was ultimately, Jefferson wrote, "deaf to the voice of justice."

All successful leaders, particularly those hoping to bring about change and to overturn the status quo, must craft a compelling vision for the future. Paint a picture of how things could be otherwise, and show everyone where they would fit into that image. Be thoroughly constructive and solution-oriented, and make very clear how you would like to solve existing and anticipated challenges.

A vision packs a more powerful punch than does a plan. To borrow words that Jefferson liked to use, a plan speaks to the head whereas a vision speaks to the heart. The plan tells us where we could go and what we could do; a compelling vision instills us with the desire and passion to make that plan a reality. A true leader is one who makes a great vision palpable.

2. *In Language "Firm and Plain"*

In the process of creating your vision, remember what Jefferson did in writing the Declaration of Independence. He endeavored to "place before mankind the common sense of the subject in terms so plain and firm as to command their assent." Or as we might say these days, he kept it simple. The goal is to reach people with a vision, not to impress or intimidate them. Present them with a clear and understandable image of the future. Originality and creativity aren't so much in demand here as is good, old-fashioned common sense and plain talking. Find a way of getting to the heart of the matter so that your vision is apparent to everyone you're trying to reach.

Thomas Jefferson was not the first to speak of natural rights or of a democratic society based on the consent of the governed. These principles were in wide circulation prior to 1776. John Adams even remarked that Jefferson's declaration "contained no new ideas" and that "it is a commonplace compilation, its sentiments hackneyed in Congress for two years before." Jefferson was also criticized for borrowing heavily from John Locke's *Second Treatise on Government*—published in 1690—with which he was intimately familiar.

While he was certainly more of a radical than Locke, Jefferson never claimed that these essential principles were unique to him. He acknowledged that he did not try to develop "new arguments never before thought of." When he sat down to put into words the reasons why the colonies were declaring their freedom from England, Jefferson aimed instead to fill his countrymen with a vision that would stir them to action. He wanted to call them to a higher ground and dare them to create a better world. His language had to be lucid, concise, and its logic self-evident to everyone who would ever read or hear it. He did what we must do: Be clear and keep it simple.

3. Accept the Challenge, Do the Work

The exchange between John Adams and Thomas Jefferson—"You do it!" "No, you do it!"—appears comical to us now. It's difficult to imagine Jefferson suggesting that someone else write the Declaration of Independence, but he accepted that challenge. And he agreed to "do as well as I can."

Leaders are not superhuman beings. More often they're people who are simply willing at one time or another to accept a challenge and do the work that needs to be done. It's not important whether they think they can do it or believe in themselves, though that always helps. What matters most is that a leader goes forward regardless. They do their best. And usually, that's more than enough.

4. Powerful Words

Some historians today insist that the Declaration of Independence enshrined a "white male passion for white liberty." In a sense, they are correct. When Jefferson wrote that "governments are instituted among men" he definitely meant men and not people, including women.

At the time Jefferson wrote the declaration, women, blacks, and Native Americans were politically invisible. Married women were not allowed to own property, and enslaved African Americans were not even entitled to enjoy an inalienable right to liberty. But the words that Jefferson wrote in 1776 took on a powerful life of their own as America and its democracy matured. Over time, the rights once reserved for white men of property have been recognized and protected for all human beings regardless of their race, gender, religion, or economic status.

"The ball of liberty is now so well in motion," Jefferson wrote, "that it will roll round the globe." Indeed it has. The revolution that Jefferson helped to start is ongoing and continues today throughout the world. The liberty at the heart of the Declaration of Independence will be a formidable force in the world as long as we are willing to stand up for the rights of ourselves and others.

Wherever individuals are being persecuted by "monkish ignorance" and tyranny, the words of Thomas Jefferson will ring clear. "The oppressed should rebel," he wrote in 1776, "and they will continue to rebel and raise disturbance until their civil rights are fully restored to them and all partial distinctions, exclusions, and incapacitations are removed."

The underlying lesson is this: Words, especially words of truth, have incredible power and must never be underestimated. They can take on a life of their own and will inspire and motivate others in your absence. A vision based on such powerful words has the potential to do more good and reach more people than you are capable of imagining in your own time.

It was Jefferson's hope that America would be to the nations of the world a model of democracy, or "republicanism" as it was then more commonly referred to. He dreamed that we would always lead the way by earnestly fanning the flames of liberty. It was his wish that the United States would govern "itself by what is wise and just for the many, uninfluenced by the local and selfish views of the few who direct their affairs." It is our challenge not only to live up to his powerful words but to surpass his greatest expectations.

5. *"Come Forward"*

The fifth principle of successful leadership that Jefferson demonstrated in writing the Declaration of Independence is, without a doubt, the most important.

As already mentioned, Thomas Jefferson was not a great public speaker. John Adams recalled, "During the whole time I sat with him in congress, I never heard him utter three sentences together." Jefferson was shy and often refrained from speaking in a crowd. It just wasn't his forte. But when it came time to pick up a pen, his talent could not be matched. Jefferson contributed in the best way he could: He wrote. The world has never been the same since.

Each one of us is gifted with talents and abilities. Sadly, many people sell themselves short. Effective leadership does not mean you should mirror someone else. It means offering your very best in a common cause with others. Once you're willing to do that, you've accepted the challenge of leadership.

Just imagine if Jefferson had said, "I'm not a good public speaker like Patrick Henry. I can't do this. I'm going home"; or if he'd said, "I'm not a good military man like George Washington. I quit." Jefferson stayed the course and waited for the opportune time when his talents could be used best. He refused to allow his lack of skill as an orator or as a military leader to keep him from seizing a position of leadership.

> **"Come forward then," Jefferson wrote, "and give us the aid of your talents and the weight of your character towards the new establishment of republicanism."**

Jefferson the Revolutionary: Some Final Thoughts

As it was for the fledgling nation, 1776 was a significant turning point for Thomas Jefferson. The young Virginian evolved from being a competent, quiet country lawyer to one of the world's most important revolutionary leaders. Jefferson came forward with unabashed, youthful passion to "set the pace" in the debate over self-government. He did not back down when others thought him "too bold." He persevered when the leaders he looked up to lacked "forwardness and zeal." He put his talents to use and helped to create a new language of freedom that is still spoken today.

If you could change one thing about the status quo of your

life, what would it be? How about your business? Your town? Are you willing to be a revolutionary and make the changes that you believe should be made? Will you question authority? Do you have a vision for how things could be? Are you willing to overcome "narrow limits" and "monkish ignorance"? Come forward then, and lead.

- Being a leader means answering the call to serve whenever it sounds. "There is a debt of service due from every man to his country."
- Are you up against "narrow limits" of "habitual belief"? Progressive leadership requires that you stay committed to thinking outside the box and remain courageous enough to stand on your convictions.
- Question authority and be willing to challenge the status quo. Think for yourself. "It behooves our citizens to be on their guard, to be firm in their principles, and full of confidence in themselves."
- Leaders seek out like-minded people with whom to coordinate their actions.
- Leadership is seldom given; it is taken by those who are willing to manifest the boldness and passion that the times require.
- Get people emotionally involved in your plan.
- Always be looking to open up new channels of communication with other groups or individuals who can help your cause.
- Make a great vision palpable. Remember, a plan speaks to the head while a vision speaks to the heart.
- Keep it simple by using common sense and language "firm and plain."
- Successful leadership relies on the fact that you accept the challenge and do the work as well as you can.

- A great vision based on powerful words has the potential to do more good and reach more people than even you can imagine in your own time.
- Leaders know that everyone has unique talents and skills to offer. Don't sell yourself short.

CHAPTER 4

JEFFERSON THE LEGISLATOR

It is comfortable to see the standard of reason at length erected, after so many ages during which the human mind has been held in vassalage by kings, priests & nobles: and it is honorable for us to have produced the first legislature who had the courage to declare that the reason of man may be trusted with the formation of his own opinions.

Thomas Jefferson's work as a Virginia legislator in the late 1770s provides us with some compelling lessons of leadership. During the three-year period 1776–79, he worked on various legislative committees to overhaul the laws that would govern the new state. His biographer Dumas Malone has written that these years represented Jefferson's "most creative period as a statesman during the American Revolution, and there was no part of his entire career that he afterward looked back upon with greater satisfaction . . . and at no other time, perhaps, was the essence of his philosophy and statesmanship so unmistakably revealed."

While George Washington and his brave troops battled the British, Jefferson took on the Virginia aristocracy and the Anglican church in the legislature. He aspired to ensure that the vision of freedom at the heart of the Declaration of Independence would not prove to be idle rhetoric, but would actually be realized in the laws of a new society. "He regarded political independence," Malone writes, "not as an end but as a means, and was more deeply concerned about what should follow the formal separation than about the action itself."

AUTHOR UNKNOWN

Contrary to what many people now believe, fame did not come to Jefferson after he wrote the Declaration of Independence in the summer of 1776. Aside from a small circle of colleagues and friends, no one even knew Jefferson was the author. That fact was not brought out until 1783 when his authorship was mentioned in a sermon that was then published in a pamphlet in New England.

But the fact that Jefferson had written the illustrious document was not widely known until the late 1790s, twenty years after the fact, when his supporters used it as a way to promote him in his bid for the presidency. Until his old age Jefferson politely downplayed his role in the Declaration of Independence to avoid seeming like a self-promoter.

As the summer of 1776 wound to a close, congressional delegates continued to add their names to the declaration. In late August the British pushed General Washington and his troops out of New York, across New Jersey, and into Pennsylvania. Months afterward, in December of that year, Washington crossed the Delaware River and surprised the British at Trenton, in a stealth maneuver in which he took almost a thousand prisoners.

From our vantage point over two hundred years later, the Americans seem to have been destined for success. But at the time, it was not at all certain how things would turn out. Washington's ragtag colonial militia was up against the strongest, best-equipped army in the entire world. The odds were against an American victory from the outset. Jefferson and his cohorts who masterminded the revolution were branded as traitors and rebels. If captured, they would have been hauled to England in chains, imprisoned, and quite possibly executed.

Approximately a third of all Americans didn't even support the revolution at all. These loyalists—Tories, as they were known—saw the fracas not as a revolution but as a civil war instigated by power-hungry extremists spouting mumbo jumbo about inalienable rights and liberty. In the summer of 1776 little was certain except that the young republic had crossed a threshold.

"MAN OF ACTION"

One other thing was definite in August 1776: Thomas Jefferson wanted to go home. With another Continental Congress gearing up to hold meetings, Jefferson was still in Philadelphia representing Virginia, but his mind was elsewhere.

Back in Williamsburg a legislative assembly was preparing to convene in October to consider an original constitution and new set of laws to govern the state. Jefferson wanted badly to be there. As he recalled: "I knew that our legislation under the regal government had many very vicious points which urgently required reformation, and I thought I could be of more use in forwarding that work."

After repeated appeals, Jefferson was finally replaced with a new delegate in Congress and resigned his seat in early September. He eagerly packed his things and headed home to Monticello. A few weeks later, his wife, Martha, traveled with him to Williamsburg, where he took his seat in the Virginia House of Delegates on October 7, 1776.

Historian and biographer Bernard Mayo has observed that over the next three years Jefferson the idealist "became the man of action, the leader of a bloodless social revolution." With the vision of the Declaration of Independence firmly in place,

Jefferson got down to the nitty-gritty of legislation: What exactly should the laws be in a free society? How much freedom should the law allow? How far should the government go in protecting the natural rights of its citizens? These were questions the Virginia delegates were charged with answering. And Jefferson definitely had some responses to give.

WHERE SHOULD YOU BE?

Jefferson instinctively recognized that he needed to be there when the legislative assembly met in Williamsburg in the autumn of 1776. Make no mistake, he could easily have stayed in Philadelphia and coasted through more meetings of the Continental Congress. The leaders in the Virginia Assembly weren't exactly begging him to come home.

Philadelphia was a big city with a lot going on. There were always plenty of parties and dinners to enjoy in the evenings. His duties in the Congress demanded much less of his energies than would the legislative work in Virginia. Granted, he missed his wife, Martha, terribly. But all in all, he could have opted to stay in Philadelphia for a while longer and enjoy himself. But he chose not to.

Jefferson fought to come home and take part in the hard work of crafting a new government in his home state because he knew that that is where he could, as he said, "be of more use." He did it for two reasons: First, by this time he was keenly aware of where his skills and talents lay. He was a competent researcher and an excellent writer. And those were some of the very contributions the assembly would need most when it came to writing the new laws that would govern the Virginia commonwealth. Second, and more important, Jefferson was cognizant of the fact that if left to their own devices, the older and more conservative aristocrats in the assembly would not go far enough in making the kind of changes that he felt should be made. The legislature needed a young progressive to push the envelope and challenge their traditionalist views. Without that, a successful revolution would mean nothing more than replacing a British monarchy with a Virginian aristocracy. And that's not why Jefferson had become a revolutionary. As he once wrote, "An elective despotism was not the government we fought for."

He had to be in those meetings and weigh in on the debates so that he could make sure the vision in the Declaration of Independence would be realized. Virginia, he believed, would be the example for the rest of the country. It would be a laboratory for democracy where the benefits of freedom and Enlightenment would be enjoyed. He wanted to see his home state, with his help, take the vanguard in establishing a new society.

A diligent leader cannot simply lay out a vision and expect every one else to make it happen. He or she has to be willing to get down in the trenches and do the grunt work to realize the vision's true potential.

Pause for a moment and ask yourself: Are you where you need to be so that you can "be of more use"? Take a good look around—are you in the ideal spot where your talents and skills can have the most effect? Where are you investing most of your time and energy? Is it paying off for you and your family? for your business? for your community? Have you been idling away somewhere, out of the loop, when you should really be hard at work helping to create a new vision? Have you been avoiding doing the grunt work?

Figure out where you need to be so that your efforts can have the most results—where you can be of most benefit to yourself and to others. Then get there as fast as you can. Don't sit around and wait for someone to make your vision a reality. It's not going to happen. You have to be the one to get that ball rolling.

GET RESULTS

Before we explore Jefferson's legislative work in detail, let's consider a few of the more general principles of leadership that he showcased during his period as a lawmaker. Foremost among them was his pragmatic concern with results. Jefferson could certainly be an idealist. He was infinitely positive about human nature and about the future of democracy in America and the world. He honestly felt that humankind was awakening from a deep sleep, refreshed and ready to eradicate tyranny and injustice. In his heart, he was a romantic optimist.

But at the same time, Jefferson was a devoted realist. He knew that none of the ideals of a free government would reach fruition in America if people like him weren't willing to stand and fight for them. No other leader at the time was more heedful of the fact that corruption and tyranny were always waiting in the wings; that some individuals, motivated by greed or ego, would forever strive to grab the reins of power for personal gain.

"Bribery corrupts them," he once wrote about the weakness of elected officials. "Personal interests lead them astray from the general interest of their constituents." He was sincerely concerned, he wrote, that such representatives in America might "form the most corrupt government on earth, if the means of their corruption be not prevented." In 1776 the Virginia

Assembly was for Jefferson the central forum where the struggle had begun to build an honest government that would be true to the principles of the revolution.

Ultimately the Boston Tea Party, Lexington and Concord, the Declaration of Independence, every meeting of the Virginia Assembly, and the bloody war itself then raging through the colonies were about obtaining results—securing not the mere promise of liberty but real freedom itself.

Jefferson truly believed that good government served a purpose—that it could reach positive ends. Rights could be recognized and protected. An equitable and just society could be created. The purpose of a government was not to rein in but to give free rein. Irrefutable results like these were the consummate goals throughout Jefferson's public life.

The leader of any group must always be the one most focused on results—on getting them, keeping them, and building on them.

OPPORTUNITY: TAKE IT NOW

Successful leadership depends in no small way on your willingness to seize on an opportunity for all it is worth. That was precisely what these early years spent creating a new state government were to Jefferson. He recognized the era that he lived in as a unique moment in history, one offering an incredible opportunity to effect substantial changes in society. Thereafter, as the country matured, change would be harder to come by. Jefferson knew what all leaders know: We should be prepared to strike when the iron is hot; we should not hesitate to seize an opportunity when we're convinced the time is right. As he later wrote,

> It can never be too often repeated that the time for fixing every essential right on a legal basis is while our rulers are honest, and ourselves united. From the conclusion of this war we shall be going down hill. It will not then be necessary to resort every moment to the people for support. They will be forgotten therefore, and their rights disregarded. They will forget themselves, but in the sole faculty of making money, and will never think of uniting to effect a due respect for their rights. The shackles, therefore, which shall not be knocked off at the conclusion of this war, will remain on us long, will be made heavier and heavier, till our rights shall revive or expire in convulsion.

STAND YOUR GROUND

Thomas Jefferson was driven during his work as a legislator by what historian Joyce Appleby describes as a

> profound antagonism to the debasing effects of tyranny. . . . He carried to his death his hostility to authoritarian doctrines, precedents, and officials. But Jefferson was more than a catalyst for the liberal opinions rife in society, he was the live wire that made the connection between Enlightenment philosophy and American public policy.

That live wire was certainly hot in the years that Jefferson served in the Virginia Assembly. He was up against some serious opposition, though. Appleby observes that most of the men Jefferson served with were "socially conservative and intellectually unadventurous." Thomas Jefferson, on the other hand, was a bold thinker, open to new ideas, and not afraid to stand up to convention.

Many of Jefferson's actions in the Assembly were met with bitter hostility by some of the wealthy landowners and clergy. Despite his powerful opponents, Jefferson stood his ground and refused to back down. While older, perhaps more experienced politicians criticized him for his views and chided him as being too aggressive with reforms, he persisted nonetheless.

"Only lay down true principles," Jefferson once wrote, "and adhere to them inflexibly. Do not be frightened into their surrender by the alarms of the timid, or the croakings of wealth against the ascendancy of the people."

INFLUENCE, DON'T DOMINATE

As a Virginia legislator, Jefferson demonstrated a discerning approach to power that he would rely on throughout his political career. He determined not to control the meetings of the Assembly or the actions of his fellow representatives—which it's likely the thirty-three-year-old couldn't have done anyway. He resolved rather to infuse the legislation he worked on and the spirit of the debates that he took part in with his own vision. In the words of Dumas Malone:

> It would be too much to claim that he dominated the legislative scene; but unquestionably he assumed a position of great influence at the outset and largely maintained it during the sessions that followed. He was able to influence because he had effected in his own person a rare blend of the qualities of a prophet and those of a practical statesman. The prophetic

role appears the greater in the perspective of history, and his contemporaries could hardly have failed to glimpse it. To them however he also appeared as one who was engaged in the humdrum tasks of legislation. He was ceaselessly industrious and bore his full share of legislative routine.

THE RIGHT BALANCE OF PROPHET AND STATESMAN

Like Thomas Jefferson, effective leaders combine the "qualities of a prophet" (sharing their vision) with the skills of "a practical statesman" (advocating a workable plan). By contrast, ineffective and even dangerous leaders hope to sway others through pure domination or coercion. They typically display either too much of the prophet and not enough of the statesman, or vice versa. It is completely out of balance. Successfully applied, the formula relies on a delicate harmony that is constantly adjusted as conditions change.

SHORT-TERM GOALS, LONG-TERM REWARD

Jefferson knew that a republican society based on democratic principles would not manifest itself overnight. The laws that he wrote and fought for in the Virginia Assembly represented short-term changes that he believed would effect beneficial reforms in the long run. The Bill for Religious Freedom, a change in inheritance laws, a bill to create a publicly funded school system, and his bill against slavery—all were relatively short-term proposals that would, in his view, strengthen democracy in America as the country grew.

It's true that not all of his proposals were accepted. In many respects Jefferson was years ahead of his time. But he and his supporters—George Mason and James Madison among them—struggled diligently in the Virginia Assembly against the opposition of the old order. In the end, Jefferson hoped to put Virginia on a specific track, headed down a certain course into the future—a path that optimized freedom, justice, and social mobility.

Manageable, short-term goals focus our attention and efforts. Leaders appreciate and make clear the link between these goals and the long-term rewards that will result.

"A NATURAL ARISTOCRACY"

Just three days after the Assembly convened, Jefferson submitted his proposal for a law that would establish a new court system in Virginia. The reform package eventually passed. He pushed for more humane treatment of criminals and for stepping up efforts at rehabilitation instead of continuing to rely on severe punishments. He took a stand to limit the use of the death penalty. He argued in favor of term limits for office holders because, without them, he felt strongly that America would be vulnerable to the establishment of a monarchy and permanent ruling class.

Jefferson put himself at odds with the Virginia aristocracy when he proposed new legislation that would change inheritance and property laws. He was trying to break up the remnants of English feudalism in America and make it easier for more people to get ahead. The gentry and wealthy landowners attacked him as a "traitor to his class."

For Thomas Jefferson it was a simple matter. As long as the wealthy few exerted undue influence on society, enjoying freedoms, privileges, and advantages the rest of the country did not (as they had always done under the British system), then the promise of a democratic revolution would never be fully realized. "That liberty [is pure] which is to go to all," Jefferson declared, "and not to the few or the rich alone."

The young legislator believed that government, as the instrument of action for the majority will of the people, must take the lead by laying the foundations for equality. This meant new laws that would extend the right to vote among men less privileged, give land to those who didn't own any, prevent rich families from stockpiling their wealth in enormous estates, limit the amount of land that the wealthy could own, and create publicly funded schools that disseminated educational opportunities throughout all levels of society—all of which were measures that Jefferson supported.

Rivals naturally decried the young progressive's initiatives. Wealthy planter Landon Carter complained to his friend George Washington that Jefferson was waging an attack on the "right to do as we please with our own property." But Jefferson continued to fight the battle, as one historian observed, to "set an aristocratic society in the current of democracy by broadening its economic base."

For Jefferson, America was full of promising individuals of great talents and character who never got a chance to rise to prominence and make a contribution to society because the rigid, tradition-bound class system inherited from England promoted only an affluent few. He described the situation in a letter to John Adams:

> I agree with you that there is a natural aristocracy among men. The grounds of this are virtue and talents. . . . There is also an artificial aristocracy founded on wealth and birth, without either virtue or talents. The natural aristocracy I consider as the most precious gift of nature for the instruction, the trusts, and government of society. . . . The artificial

aristocracy is a mischievous ingredient in government, and provision should be made to prevent its ascendancy.

Until the end of his life Jefferson argued that the door must be held open to allow the best and brightest to come forward and make their mark. Only by encouraging the finest from every individual could America become the beacon of liberty to the world. During his years as a lawmaker he demonstrated a belief that government should take steps to ensure that the door is always held open to future leaders, be they rich or poor.

Jefferson's approach to government assumed that the cultivation of leadership was utterly crucial. No longer would society depend on a few well-to-do families for leadership. Every citizen would be called on to contribute as best they could to the success of this great experiment in democracy called America.

What about you? Are you doing what you can as a leader to find and encourage the natural aristocracy of virtue and talent in your organization? in your community? Are you helping to hold that door open so that the best and brightest can emerge? Are you cultivating new leadership? Or are you holding on to a traditional way of doing things, coddling an artificial aristocracy that no longer warrants special treatment?

"THE MEANS OF DEVELOPMENT"

Thomas Jefferson had been raised in a society that valued wealth and privilege over character, merit, and talent. It was his goal as a lawmaker to reverse that fundamental bias. He knew that the best and the brightest the country had to offer would not emerge as long as education and opportunity were limited to a narrow upper class. It was the proper role of the Virginia Assembly, as he saw it, to create a publicly funded school system that made education available to all classes of white society. To that end, Jefferson introduced his Bill for the General Diffusion of Knowledge, certainly one of the most radical proposals he ever made as a legislator.

The goal of the bill, as he described it, was "to bring into action that mass of talents which lies buried in poverty in every country for want of the means of development." A precursor to public education in America as we know it, his plan included a tiered network of schools: elementary schools for children (white boys and girls), secondary schools for older boys, and a state college for truly promising young men. Though his initial design wasn't the hallmark of equality as we'd define it today (only white male students who performed well in classes would have the opportunity to further their education as they grew older), the proposal represented a drastic transformation from the traditional system then in place.

One of the most controversial elements of the legislation was funding. Jefferson recognized at the outset that the wealthier members of the Virginia Assembly would likely object to using the state treasury to educate underprivileged children. He knew that many politicians would rather spend public money to invest in commerce than in schools for kids. "People generally have more feeling for canals and roads than education," he once lamented. "However, I hope we can advance them with equal pace."

As with other issues that were important to him, Jefferson was fighting a conventional way of doing things that powerful interests weren't eager to see changed. Members of the clergy didn't like his proposal to loosen their grip on education in Virginia. In addition to that, schooling had always been a private matter for those who could afford it—a luxury for the rich alone. Asking the state to step in and assume that responsibility to the benefit of poorer families was a radical proposition.

Some at the time viewed it as an extravagant measure, firm in their belief that education was better left to the private sector. It was for some—to use a modern-day phrase—nothing but a "big government" scheme that forced the rich to spend their money to help the poor. Many legislators were less than enthusiastic about it, and saw it as yet another Jefferson-led attack on the affluent and the clergy. Action on the bill was delayed for many years due to a lack of funding and opposition to its grandiosity. When it did pass the assembly, many years later, it had been whittled down considerably and scarcely resembled its original form. Jefferson was disappointed.

"CRUSADE AGAINST IGNORANCE"

Underlying Jefferson's reform package was his conviction that a general education was absolutely essential to the success of a free society. How can we expect people to take part in the decisions of government if they are not educated? As Jefferson argued,

> Every government degenerates when trusted to the rulers of the people alone. The people themselves, therefore, are its only safe depositories. And to render even them safe, their minds must be improved to a certain degree.

Because the very health of the republic depended on the "diffusion of knowledge" among the people, Jefferson was adamant that it was the proper duty of the state to make sure it was done right. A healthy government and the educational system it would rely on were much too important to leave to the "accidental circumstances of wealth or birth." Jefferson wrote to his mentor, George Wythe, in 1786,

> I think by far the most important bill in our whole code is that for the diffusion of knowledge among the people. No other sure foundation can be devised for the preservation of freedom and happiness. . . . Preach, my dear Sir, a crusade against ignorance; establish and improve the law for educating the common people. . . . The tax which will be paid for this purpose is not more than the thousandth part of what will be paid to kings, priests, and nobles who will rise up among us if we leave the people in ignorance.

"A WALL OF SEPARATION"

One of Thomas Jefferson's most notable achievements as a Virginia legislator was his Bill for Religious Freedom, which he wrote in 1777. He admitted later that this was "the most controversial subject" with which he was ever involved. Aside from the Declaration of Independence, he considered this statute as the most important accomplishment in his entire life. It preceded the First Amendment to the U.S. Constitution by more than a decade.

The groundbreaking document spelled out the nature of a free religious practice and the role of personal faith in a democratic republic. Religion for Jefferson was a tremendously private affair. "I have ever thought religion a concern purely between our God and our consciences," he wrote, "for which we were accountable to Him and not to the priests." As they did with many of Jefferson's other proposals, some Virginia delegates thought the bill was too extreme, and they passionately opposed it. But with help from his supporters the legislation was at last signed into law in 1786, after almost ten years of debate.

To appreciate just how radical Jefferson's Bill for Religious Freedom truly was and why it generated such fierce opposition, we need to understand the world in which he lived. As one writer has perceptively observed, the past is like a foreign country—people did things differently there. Religious life in eighteenth-century America can definitely attest to that.

Jefferson grew up in a world in which the Anglican church was as powerful a force in people's lives as the government. The church and the state were soundly united. A newborn child was automatically considered a member of the Church. Individuals could be fined or even jailed for not supporting the clergy or attending services. And people's taxes could be used to support the Church, whether they were believers or not. For someone like Jefferson—who believed there was a profound difference between a personal faith in God and the dogma of any church—the situation ran contrary to the Enlightenment ideals of free thought that he championed.

Not only that, but Jefferson saw the church's power over humankind as unadulterated tyranny—no different from the unchecked despotism of the British monarchy or the authoritarianism of the wealthy aristocracy that controlled parliament. He declared in 1800, "I have sworn upon the altar of god, eternal hostility against every form of tyranny over the mind of man." That much-quoted remark was made in specific reference to the church. As long as the government and church worked in tandem to coerce citizens to accept specific tenets of faith, Thomas Jefferson viewed such actions as an abuse of power and a corruption of the public trust.

Though he remained throughout his life a steadfast supporter of the moral philosophy of Jesus, Jefferson believed that church leaders had corrupted those teachings with superstition and mysticism. In an 1810 letter he reiterated his defiant stand that the teachings of Jesus were "the purest system of morals ever before preached to man," but that priests have "perverted" them "into an engine for enslaving mankind" and used them "to filch wealth and power to themselves."

Thomas Jefferson was resolute in his belief that a free society should steadfastly maintain "a wall of separation between church and state"—a metaphor that he coined in 1802. That meant public schools were to have "no religious reading, instruction, or exercise"; that by law no one would be "compelled to frequent or support any religious worship, place, or ministry whatsoever." Jefferson's Virginia Statute for Religious Freedom stood solidly for both a freedom of religion privately practiced and a freedom from religion imposed by government. When the bill was finally signed into law, Jefferson proudly commented:

> It is comfortable to see the standard of reason at length erected, after so many ages during which the human mind has been held in vassalage by kings, priests & nobles: and it is honorable for us to have produced the first legislature who had the courage to declare that the reason of man may be trusted with the formation of his own opinions.

Needless to say, Jefferson's views were out of step with those of many Americans at the time. His opponents—including political conservatives and numerous members of the clergy—viciously attacked him in the press, erroneously describing him as an atheist and anti-religious zealot. Later, when he won the presidency, it was said that hysterical women across New England buried their bibles in their gardens and hid them in wells for fear that President Jefferson would order the books burned.

In reality, Thomas Jefferson was not at all opposed to religious faith and worship, and he is rightly recognized as one of the most spiritual presidents America has ever had. In his later years he personally supported Unitarianism and was optimistic that it would become the primary faith of the United States. He drew the line, however, when it came to organized religion exerting political influence in society.

At the root of Jefferson's progressive views on religious freedom are a confidence in the ability of the individual to think for himself and a stalwart faith in an appeal to tolerance. As a leader, Jefferson appreciated and valued the diversity of a free-thinking public. "It does me no injury," he once wrote, "for my neighbor to say that there are twenty gods or no god. It neither picks my pocket nor breaks my leg." He was not intimidated by someone's devout views, so long as he wasn't coerced to adopt them.

"WHO WILL NOT BEND"

As a Virginia lawmaker in the late 1770s, Jefferson demonstrated his commitment to making good on the vision of liberty in the Declaration of Independence. He took a stand against convention and led the vanguard in laying the foundation for an honest and effective state government that would be a model for the nation. With that goal in mind, he combined his talents as a writer and philosopher with his skill as a politician to push for radical legislation—much of which was ahead of its time.

It is a popular misconception that Jefferson said "that government is best which governs least." That statement was actually made by journalist John L. O'Sullivan a decade after Jefferson's death. While it's true that Jefferson was emphatically opposed to government exercising too much power—for fear that it would trample on the rights and liberties of its citizens—he was just as much against government exercising too little. Ever the advocate of moderation, he once wrote that "we are now vibrating between too much and too little government, and the pendulum will rest finally in the middle."

For Jefferson, an honest but limited government empowered by the will of the people had the ability to do great things for society—uppermost among them being the protection of our rights against forces that would profit from their elimination.

At the same time, however, he was realistic enough to know that those in public office—naturally disposed to desiring greater power and wealth—were easily corrupted, and a corrupt government inevitably devolves into tyranny, at which point government begins to work against the very rights it was created to protect.

The success of a democratic government will therefore always depend on scrupulous leaders of strong character. Jefferson wrote, "I love to see honest and honorable men at the helm who will not bend their politics to their purses nor pursue measures by which they may profit and then profit by their measures." Jefferson's formula for successful government rested squarely on cultivating principled leadership—both in public office and among the people.

Many of Thomas Jefferson's contemporaries criticized him—just as some people might today—for having too much faith in the positive side of human nature. But he remained confident that good government was always possible if the door was held open for good leaders to come forward. Then, as now, his optimism was inspiring.

Jefferson the Legislator: Some Final Thoughts

Still in his mid-thirties, Thomas Jefferson represented a new generation of leadership in Virginia in the 1770s. Though his political adversaries were not always in agreement with the boldness of his proposals, they respected the young man's intelligence and talents, and were impressed by his tenacity.

As revealed during these years in the Virginia General Assembly, Jeffersonian leadership stands for merit over privilege, free thought against dogma, virtue over greed, and progressive change against convention. Tolerance for the views of others, support for educational opportunities and social mobility, and a determined resolve to cultivate new leadership are also central themes.

- Are you where you need to be to "be of more use"? Are your skills and talents being put to best use? Is it paying off for you and your family?
- Leaders don't wait for others to make their vision a reality. They lead by example, not afraid to do the work and get the ball rolling.
- Stay focused on the results of your efforts. Don't be content with rhetoric. A leader is ever hungry for results—getting them, keeping them, and building on them.
- Your life is made up of a multitude of unique moments offering incredible opportunities. Seize them when the moment is right.
- Stand your ground in support of the "true principles" in which you believe. As Thomas Jefferson said, "Do not be frightened into their surrender by the alarms of the timid."
- Effective leaders seek to influence the actions of others, not dominate them. Infuse the debate and help to craft an agenda that reflects the vision behind your plan.
- Train your energies and efforts on accomplishing short-term goals that each contribute to a long-term reward.
- Stay committed to finding the "natural aristocracy"—the best and the brightest—in any organization or team. Call them forward to join you in accepting the mantle of leadership. Refuse to coddle an "artificial aristocracy" that no longer deserves the privileges it enjoys.
- In whatever venue you find yourself, lead a crusade against ignorance. Improve the opportunities all members of your team have to educate themselves and sharpen their skills.

- Leadership means being aware that others have personal faiths and beliefs that you may not share and being sensitive to it. That should not prevent people from working together as a team and focusing on worthwhile goals.
- The best leaders are those who inspire others with the courage, motivation, and freedom, not to follow, but to become leaders themselves.

CHAPTER 5

JEFFERSON THE WARRIOR

There is a time in human suffering when exceeding sorrows are but like snow falling on an iceberg.

The five-year period 1779–84 was one of the most difficult episodes in Thomas Jefferson's life. With the benefit of a solid reputation and experience from his years in the Continental Congress and in the Virginia house of delegates, Jefferson was elected governor of his native state in 1779. He had hoped to accomplish much in the position, but fate placed one obstacle after another in front of him that prevented him from realizing his goals. These years were marked by great strife and conflict in Virginia. As the governor of a state at war, the commander of a struggling army, and one of the leaders of a new country fighting for its independence, Jefferson was overwhelmed with responsibility and nearly insurmountable odds. Jefferson biographer and historian Merrill Peterson has written that "the republican convictions, easy temperament, and philosophical turn of mind that had served him so well in the legislative forums of the revolution would prove less serviceable to executive leadership in a situation fraught with disaster." Jefferson left office after two years, humiliated, and retreated to the solitude of Monticello.

As if that weren't enough, he suffered incredible personal losses as well. About this time Jefferson endured the deaths of four children and his beloved wife. He experienced a crushing period of depression and defeat. This was in many ways his darkest hour. He was a man fighting to overcome public and private adversities. In dealing with these challenges, we witness a leader brought to the brink.

GOVERNOR JEFFERSON

Jefferson was thirty-six years old when he was elected governor of Virginia by his fellow legislators on June 1, 1779. One of the younger leaders of the reform-minded faction of the Assembly, he succeeded Patrick Henry in office. Thomas and Martha Jefferson and their two daughters promptly moved into the Governor's Palace in Williamsburg. This was the same residence where, as a young student over fifteen years before, he had dined and talked philosophy with his mentors. It must have been quite exciting for him to walk through that house as the new governor. The Jeffersons later moved to a home in Richmond when the state capital was relocated there in 1780.

America had undoubtedly seen its share of suffering in the War for Independence. The British had taken New York and Philadelphia in the North and Savannah in the South. George Washington and his army had been dealt some heavy blows and had suffered through the deadly winter of 1777–78 in Valley Forge, Pennsylvania, where thousands of soldiers succumbed to the effects of bitter cold and starvation.

There was some cause for celebration, however. The army of British General Burgoyne, which had threatened to split New England from the rest of the country, finally surrendered at Saratoga, New York, in October 1777. That critical victory helped to attract assistance from France, which officially recognized America's independence a few months later. Despite the French aid, British forces continued to wreak havoc around the country.

By the time Jefferson took over as governor in the summer of 1779, Virginia was facing runaway inflation, a depleted state treasury, a scarcity of food, incredibly low morale, and the real possibility of invasion by British troops. One contemporary observer commented that "never was a country in a more shabby situation."

In terms of a political career, it was obviously not the best time to be governor. But Jefferson knew this going in. Just a few days after he accepted the post he wrote to his friend Richard Henry Lee, "In a virtuous government, and more especially in times like these, public offices are what they should be, burdens to those appointed to them, which it would be wrong to decline, though foreseen to bring with them intense labour and great private loss." In terms of leadership, Jefferson once again revealed his undying commitment to serve when called on—to put his talents to use for his country and to do the very best he could under circumstances he knew would be trying.

"BEYOND HIS CONTROL"

As governor, Jefferson was in charge of one of the largest state militias in the country, fighting a war that looked as if it might never be won. It was a position particularly challenging for the Virginian—considering the fact that he had no military experience. As a representative in congress and even as a delegate in the state assembly, he had never served on any of the committees specially charged with overseeing the needs of the army. He was every bit the novice when it came to directing and supplying a fighting force. Literally overnight Jefferson's leadership entered a new realm, and he was forced to make decisions about issues with which he had little or no previous experience.

Topping a long list of formidable concerns was Virginia's underfunded army—it lacked even the most necessary supplies like guns, food, clothing, tents, and wagons. Inflation was rampant, the treasury was empty, and taxes were neither collected nor paid. Though plenty of volunteers were willing to fight, the state had no means to equip them with the provisions they needed in battle. The brave men often showed up for service without weapons or shoes, looking for food. Jefferson wrote that "the want of money cramps every effort." Such monetary shortages would plague his difficult tenure as governor.

Virginia's soldiers, like their counterparts in other states, grew impatient waiting for supplies. They felt abandoned by their leaders—men that had promised them liberty but couldn't even give them shoes. Some indignant soldiers talked openly of a coup and pledged their loyalty to King George. Their planned insurrection never came off, though similar revolts did occur in other states.

Morale was not only horribly low at the front but at home as well. By 1779 many Virginians had grown tired of the war. There was no money, little food, and the ever-present threat of invasion. Many people felt unsafe, and there was no apparent reason to feel overly confident in Jefferson's ability as a military leader.

Compounding the problems for Jefferson was an uncooperative and bureaucratic state government that did not even meet on a regular basis. When they did, Jefferson seemed unable to provide the motivation to stir them to significant action. Just a few years before he was the master of the pen, but now he seemed lost in paperwork. He was befuddled and discouraged with the day-to-day details of fighting a war in which victory appeared to move increasingly beyond his reach. Dumas Malone remarks that Governor Jefferson

> could not have been a high-powered modern executive even if he had wanted to be one. The constitution of the state and the spirit of the times made that quite impossible. Jefferson could not have avoided trouble if he had had far greater power and wisdom, and it is hard to see how anyone could have been genuinely effective in the larger sense with the instruments which were available to his hand. . . . This was predominantly a time of frustration. The major difficulties proved to be beyond his control.

REMIND THE PEOPLE

The case could be made that Jefferson failed to provide the leadership Virginia desperately needed at that time. Granted, he occupied a relatively weak office, politically speaking, and faced a series of emergencies that would have tried any governor. He had no experience as an executive or as the leader of an army. Up to this point he had always led behind the scenes.

In all fairness, many of the problems he encountered were beyond the scope of his government to remedy or his experience to handle. Some historians have graciously concluded that Jefferson did all he could do given the circumstances against him. But did he, in light of his many talents? We can also learn lessons of leadership from the steps he did not take.

Undeniably one of Jefferson's greatest talents was writing. He had an amazing gift for creating visionary, inspiring prose. He could have put that genius to work as governor by drafting any number of public documents—declarations that would have offered his fellow Virginians some direction at a time when they needed it most. He might have written a dramatic appeal to the people for their renewed support of the war effort, reminding them of the common goal of liberty they all shared. He could have written a moving message of encouragement to the soldiers in the field, reminding them of their place in history. He could have written a document directed to the delegates in the General Assembly with recommendations about what improvements might be made to make the governor's office more effective. It's doubtful he could have written anything that would have instantly replenished the state treasury. But any effort by that marvelous writer would have been a great boost to the spirits of his people.

Perhaps we're asking too much from history. Jefferson did not have the advantage of two hundred years of hindsight that we enjoy. On a daily basis he was faced with the grim realities of war. Bogged down in administrative duties in the governor's office, he was likely too busy to devote himself to writing such documents. Besides, such direct appeals to the public by political leaders were not as common nor as easily disseminated then as they are today.

But the more essential point is this: Many people in Virginia were making terrific and painful sacrifices with no victory in sight. They had grown tired of the struggle, and were ready to pull the plug on a revolution that appeared to be going nowhere. They needed a leader to remind them why they had gone down this path in the first place—a leader who could communicate a sense of vision and purpose to help keep their determination strong and revitalize their will. Thomas Jefferson was one of the greatest communicators of his time. He was in the right place at the right time to convey these messages, but he was busy trying to find a way to get guns into the hands of his soldiers and to put shoes on their feet.

There are two important lessons to draw from this: First, people naturally grow weary in times of adversity. Their morale and sense of purpose begin to wear thin. They start to doubt themselves and their leaders. They lose sight of the goal that once seemed so clear and tangible. Unless a leader makes a direct connection between the sacrifices people are being asked to make and the common victory that lies before them, they grow less willing to keep up the struggle.

People need to be reminded that they are important and that their contributions really do matter. They also need to be reminded on a regular basis what they're fighting for—especially when times are hard. And every effort that they make, no matter how small, needs to be met with grateful appreciation. It's the duty of a leader to make sure all these things are done.

Second, when the struggle is at its worst and your efforts seem all for naught, stop and ask yourself, What do I do best? What are my talents? Am I putting them to work to win this victory? Leaders are often sidetracked into administrative details and paperwork—duties that are often not their strong suit. They find themselves working to *manage* a problem instead of grabbing the reins and leading people to *solve* the problem.

Stop, pull back, and reevaluate your situation. Reestablish your short-term goals and remind yourself what you do best. Figure out how your talents can contribute to realizing those goals and put that plan into action without delay.

All of this is not to say that Jefferson was a completely ineffective governor. In spite of the incredible odds working against his success, he displayed some remarkable instances of leadership that are worth noting.

INFORMATION: RELIABLE AND FAST

In 1780 Jefferson was alarmed to learn that the enemy was making headway in the Southern states. Neighboring North Carolina was under attack, and British commander Lord Charles Cornwallis had taken Charleston, South Carolina, in the early summer, with hopes of cutting the Deep South off from the rest of the country. With his well-fortified and experienced forces, Cornwallis, if left unchecked, posed a serious threat to Virginia.

This situation put the spotlight on one of Jefferson's most pressing problems—a dearth of information from the front. When it did come, news was usually days late and frequently unreliable. How could he be expected to make informed decisions when he wasn't receiving clear and accurate information? He was always playing catch-up with events on the battlefield.

With the British army advancing from the south, Jefferson knew he had to improve the flow of information—and fast. To help speed up the news he established a line of messengers on horseback at forty-mile intervals from Richmond to the southern front. One letter could travel 120 miles in twenty-four hours—a lightning pace for eighteenth-century America. To ensure the information was trustworthy, he handpicked a young army officer to be his eyes and ears at the other end of the line—James Monroe.

Twenty-two-year-old Monroe was a budding protégé to the governor. A native of Virginia, he had previously served in the Continental Army in the North and endured the winter at Valley Forge with General Washington. He had recently come back to Virginia to study law under Jefferson and George Wythe. This was only the first assignment of many that Jefferson would have for Monroe. Their working relationship developed into a lifelong and heartfelt friendship that helped shape the course of American history.

Besides James Monroe in the field, Governor Jefferson relied on a dependable group of advisors in Richmond to help keep him updated on the latest turn of events. Among them were his old friends John Page and John Walker, and fellow legislator James Madison of Orange County, with whom he was now beginning a long-lasting friendship.

Having to rely on dated or questionable information is one of the worst situations a leader can be in. No matter how intelligent or capable leaders are, unless they have access to the latest and most reliable news possible their power is compromised and their authority becomes ineffective.

A leader relies on the regular flow of intelligence. It's an absolute must. Without up-to-date information from reliable sources, leaders are stripped of their abilities to make quality decisions. They are relegated to guesswork and playing catch-up—a game that cannot be won.

SEE THE WHOLE GROUND

Though he was relieved to have a trusty line of communication opened to the south, Jefferson was disappointed with the first news that it brought him. In the late summer of 1780 the Southern Army, under the command of American general Horatio Gates, was dealt a crushing blow near Camden, South Carolina. Gates had led his men (including three units of the Virginia militia) southward hoping to catch Cornwallis and his troops by surprise. But Cornwallis was marching north with the same idea. On the morning of August 16 the Americans and the British surprised each other. They squared off on a wide, dusty road flanked by pine trees and swampland.

The inexperienced soldiers from Virginia were among the

first to panic. They turned and ran without firing a shot when they saw the British redcoats running up the road. Many of them even dropped their precious guns and left them there on the battlefield. Though the Americans had outnumbered the British, they were much less prepared to fight and were soundly defeated.

Cornwallis totally routed the Southern Army and seized a supply line of 170 wagons full of provisions and ammunition. Approximately one thousand Americans were killed at the Battle of Camden and about as many taken prisoner. It was the single worst defeat the Americans faced in the Revolutionary War. General Gates, who had once rivaled his friend George Washington as the top American military commander, was publicly disgraced. He was replaced by General Nathanael Greene, who proved to be a capable military tactician.

Governor Jefferson was naturally disappointed with the news of Gates' defeat in South Carolina. But he remained committed to the plan that Virginia would continue to provide as many militiamen and supplies as it could possibly muster for the armies to the north and south. In light of such devastating news he could easily have decided instead to use what resources the state had to guard its own borders and deal with problems at home—problems that definitely existed.

For example, in Virginia there was a very real threat of invasion by sea. Native Americans, fighting in support of the British, were skirmishing with farmers in the west. And there was the mounting concern over loyalist Tories—citizens who had taken up arms to help the British crush the revolution. Jefferson had many valid reasons to keep Virginia's resources right at home. But he didn't. Whenever any appeals came from General Washington in the north or Gates and Greene in the south, he did what he could to meet their needs.

Despite all the crises he had to deal with, Jefferson never took his eyes off the big picture. He stayed attentive to the needs of America first, Virginia second. In this, one of the most distressing times of his life, he displayed a telling characteristic of great leadership: Always think in terms of the whole and contributing your share to the common cause.

When the inevitable challenges arise in your life, put that Jeffersonian leadership to work by asking yourself how the situation will affect not just you but your family, your community, your team, your business. The most effective leaders take action based on a point of view that extends beyond their front porch, beyond their desk. Like a cartographer, they imagine a broader landscape and see themselves and their challenges as a part of something much larger. Jefferson once referred to this approach as being able to "command a view of the whole ground."

ENDURE THE "HURRY, BUSTLE, AND NONSENSE"

A few weeks after the disaster at Camden, Governor Jefferson was all but ready to resign and go home. He confided to friends that he wanted desperately to retire even before his term had ended. He yearned for some peace and quiet. Autumn was coming, and on the Blue Ridge the leaves were beginning to turn. Soon they would paint the horizon with brilliant reds and ambers. The nights would grow colder, and the cool westerly winds would begin to rustle the trees at Monticello. Jefferson longed to be there.

He wished that another candidate more experienced with

military matters might take over. He felt as if he had done everything he could do, and he was out of ideas. Why stay in office when someone else might be able to do a better job? Jefferson's friends George Mason and John Page firmly urged him to stay the course.

Page wrote him, "I know your love of study and retirement must strongly solicit you to leave the hurry, bustle, and nonsense your station daily exposes you to. I know too the many mortifications you must meet with, but . . . deny yourself your darling pleasures." Loyal to his sense of duty, Jefferson took the advice of his closest friends and remained in the fray. Each day he tried to figure out how to work miracles.

He withstood the "hurry, bustle, and nonsense" of the nearly impossible job because he knew people were looking to him for leadership. It was almost that simple. He may not have liked that fact, and may have wanted to forget it and race home to Monticello. But he didn't. He stayed at his post. He stood his ground and kept trying to make things work. When nearly every sign pointed to defeat and failure, Governor Thomas Jefferson kept working for victory.

This is a dimension of executive leadership that Jefferson may not have experienced as a legislator working on committees in the state government. It was something new to him. But after almost two years in the governor's office doing his part to win a war, he was intimately familiar with it. Whether you are the head of a company, captain of a team, mayor of your city, or even a club president, executive leadership can be terribly lonely and intensely frustrating. You may get criticism for failing when you were expecting praise for trying. There may be moments when you feel as if the only positive action you have left to take is to resign.

But remember Jefferson's lesson: As long as you are in that position you represent something greater than yourself. It's no longer just about you or your abilities. It's about upholding the promise of your office. For many people, you symbolize hope and possibility. You must be willing to sacrifice your personal comfort to keep that optimism alive for others.

Leaders stand firm even though they might believe they can't go on because they know they're standing for others, not just themselves. Thomas Jefferson did what great leaders have always done—he endured.

Responsibility is neither convenient nor easy. At times being a leader will demand everything you've got, and then some. It will push you, physically and emotionally, and force you to discover a fortitude you may not have known you possessed. The triumphs and successes you may have enjoyed in the past do not make you invincible in the present or the future. Unforeseen circumstances can appear to overwhelm you with incredible odds. How you respond at these times will determine what kind of a leader you really are. In the end, adversity is the ultimate test of true leadership. Will you pack your bags and go home? Or will you endure?

STRUGGLING TO WIN

As 1780 wound to a close and the new year dawned, the situation in Virginia went from bad to worse. The event many had long feared—an invasion of British warships—finally arrived in January 1781. A force under the command of traitor Benedict Arnold sailed up the James River and sacked Richmond, burned buildings and homes, and sent the legislature scattering. What few weapons the state had were seized or destroyed, and stores of gun powder were dumped into the river. Many of Thomas Jefferson's public documents and records were torched. Arnold and his troops then sailed back down the James and set up a winter camp at Portsmouth. They made plans to join Cornwallis and his forces, who were then marching across North Carolina, gearing up to invade Virginia from the south.

Many Virginians blamed Governor Jefferson for the attack: He should have done something more; he should have been better prepared; he should have organized more resistance. Jefferson took the criticisms with decorum and went about picking up the pieces of another public embarrassment. He was angry, disappointed, and awash in crippling frustration.

On April 13, 1781, Thomas Jefferson turned thirty-eight. A real possibility existed at that point that he would be spending his next birthday in a prison in England. Two days later his new baby daughter died. It was hard to imagine things getting any worse, but they soon did. A few short weeks later he was forced to flee the capital again as British troops came tearing into the city, bent on capturing him.

THE BRITISH ARE COMING

Expecting Lord Charles Cornwallis and his mighty army to swoop down on Richmond at any time, Jefferson and the Virginia Assembly abandoned the capital in mid May. They scurried west into the mountains and reconvened in Charlottesville, where they believed themselves to be safe from the threat of invasion. A couple of weeks later Jefferson wrote to General Washington, imploring him to bring his army south and save Virginia. But the general, facing challenges of his own in the north, could not come to the rescue. He did send one of his protégés, the young French general Marquis de Lafayette, with a force of men to see what they could do, but they were no match for the combined forces of Lord Cornwallis and Benedict Arnold.

Knowing the colonials would not expect such a move, Cornwallis dispatched Colonel Banastre Tarleton and his notorious infantry to hunt down Jefferson and the rebel delegates in Charlottesville. They would have surely been captured too, if not for the quick thinking of one man, Captain John "Jack" Jouett, the South's own Paul Revere. The son of a Charlottesville innkeeper, Jouett just happened to be at Cuckoo Tavern in Louisa County, where, on the night of June 3, 1781, he saw the British dragoons stop to water their horses. He snuck out and jumped on his own horse and rode the forty miles through the night ahead of them to warn the Governor.

Early the next morning he climbed the mountain to Monticello and alerted Jefferson of the approaching British infantry before riding down into Charlottesville to notify the others. Thanks to Jouett, Jefferson, his family, and most of the other state legislators in town had enough of a warning to avoid capture. The delegates retreated west over the Blue Ridge, into the Shenandoah Valley, where they held their meetings in the small town of Staunton. Jefferson, however, was not among them.

That very weekend Jefferson's term as governor at last expired, and he happily stepped down with no intention of running again. He afterward wrote that he was "unprepared by his line of life and education for the command of armies" and that he "believed it right not to stand in the way of talents better fitted than his own to the circumstances under which the country was placed." A few days later the legislature voted General Thomas Nelson, then head of the state militia, to assume the office of governor.

"A WOUND ON MY SPIRIT"

Jefferson was scapegoated in the wake of Tarleton's raid on Charlottesville and what many saw as a humiliating retreat. Virginia had been invaded, its capital plundered and burned, and its legislature chased into the hills. As historian Virginius Dabney has written, the state was racked with "widespread exhaustion and pessimism." The British had the upper hand, and by most accounts, it appeared that they were going to win the war. Cornwallis and his forces were entrenched at Yorktown, near Williamsburg, and there was no formidable opposition in sight.

All of this took place on Jefferson's watch, and not surprisingly, many people blamed him for the dismal state of affairs. Angry Virginians branded him a coward and a failure as a leader. His political opponents in the state assembly even called for an official investigation into his conduct as governor. Jefferson would later write to his dear friend and protégé James Monroe that this inquiry "inflicted a wound on my spirit which will only be cured by the all-healing grave."

Jefferson withstood this demeaning investigation and vicious character assassination through the summer of 1781. He watched as his promising career was assaulted by rumors of incompetence. And he beheld a hopeful revolution for liberty turn into a bloody war that his country seemed fated to lose.

Faced with this very public defeat, Jefferson withdrew to the solitude and privacy of Monticello. He had had enough. He buried himself in his books, farming, and enjoyed time with his family. He and Martha planned to have another baby. He walked along the mountaintop and fed tame deer from his hand. He rode his horse across the countryside that he had explored as a child. And he busied himself writing the only book he ever produced, *Notes on the State of Virginia,* which was published a few years later. Jefferson threw himself into work he enjoyed in the place he loved: writing, research, and discovery in the mountains of Virginia. It was wonderfully therapeutic.

WHERE IS YOUR MONTICELLO?

Jefferson's experiences offer two valuable lessons there for us all. First, problems are going to arise in anyone's life, and most especially in the lives of those who step forward to assume positions of leadership. It is inevitable. Pain, sorrow, defeat, and failure can pile up and threaten any one of us. Leaders, because they are willing to bear responsibility for others, are especially vulnerable.

With that in mind, we each need a safe haven to which we can go to rest, to enjoy the quiet, to be alone, or to spend time with those we love. We each need a place to heal. Jefferson had Monticello, and later his country retreat, Poplar Forest. While on a diplomatic mission to Paris, he even rented a room in a monastery now and then just so he had a peaceful place to get away.

But not all of us can afford a mountaintop estate with a view of the Blue Ridge. In our own ways we need to carve out some space and time in our lives where we can go for reflection and repose. For some it is a cabin by the lake, for others, a garden or favorite park or library; others have a quiet room in their home for meditation.

No matter how you choose to do it, create a sanctuary for yourself where you can go and get away from the trials of the day and nourish your spirit.

Second, when you are nearly overwhelmed with defeat, throw yourself into work that you are good at and that you truly enjoy. This will renew your confidence and strength. For Jefferson it was reading and writing. For others it may be painting, cooking, fishing, gardening, working in a woodshop, or even doing crossword puzzles. It doesn't matter what it is so long as it is active work you love doing and that gives you a sense of pride and accomplishment. Sadly, too many people today seek solace in the incessant blather of a television or at the bottom of a bottle. Rather than nurturing and uplifting the spirit, such escapism does nothing but erode it.

VICTORY AT LAST

In his diary in the spring of 1781 George Washington bemoaned the sad state of affairs: "Scarce any State in the Union has, at this hour, an eighth part of its quota in the field and little prospect that I can see of ever getting more than half. . . . Instead of having the prospect of a glorious offensive campaign before us, we have a bewildered and gloomy defensive one." But that summer, while Jefferson tried to shield himself from public derision at Monticello, the winds of fate began to turn. It's as if the entire war suddenly turned on a dime.

Under direction from King Louis XVI of France, the French navy joined the American colonists just in time. By coordinating its actions with General Washington and other American and French generals on land—who brought their armies quickly south in a brilliant ruse—Cornwallis and his forces were surprised and cornered at Yorktown in the final campaign of the war.

The British surrendered on October 19, 1781. Though they would continue to occupy New York for another two years until a peace treaty had been signed, the war was over. The great struggle for independence—which many Americans just weeks before had believed all but lost—ended in a triumph for liberty.

"PAINFUL AND THANKLESS"

It's a shame Jefferson wasn't in the governor's office to enjoy the spoils of victory, after having worked so hard for two years to make it possible. He deserved to experience a form of redemption, but such is the nature of leadership. No matter how hard you work or what sacrifices you make, you may simply not be the leader at the helm when victory is achieved. Your tenure might have been the more demanding one of struggle and persistence. Thomas Jefferson understood that all too well.

Thanks to the success at Yorktown, the state legislature's punitive investigation of Jefferson lost all its steam. By the end of the year he was exonerated of any misdoings. Many Virginians began to see that despite the failings of his tenure, he had actually helped to steer them through the most difficult part of the war. His opponents continued to find fault with him, however, and his two years as governor of Virginia would haunt him for the rest of his political career.

The experience influenced him in profound ways. He had learned hard lessons about what it means to be a leader and had paid a high price in his reputation and peace of mind. He would afterward always be somewhat reluctant to accept a position of executive leadership. He later wrote, "I have no ambition to govern men. It is a painful and thankless office."

As governor he'd also learned to think differently about war. He now knew firsthand the tragedy and waste that it truly is. Though he remained certain that American independence had demanded it, he hoped the United States would thereafter avoid the siren call of war. He wrote in his *Notes on Virginia*:

> It should be our endeavour to cultivate the peace and friendship of every nation, even of that which has injured us most. . . . Never was so much false arithmetic employed to persuade nations that it is their interest to go to war. Were the

money which it has cost to gain, at the close of a long war, a little town, or a little territory, the right to cut wood here, or to catch fish there, expended in improving what they already possess, in making roads, opening rivers, building ports, improving the arts, and finding employment for their idle poor, it would render them much stronger, much wealthier and happier. This I hope will be our wisdom.

"MY DEAR WIFE"

In May 1782 Martha Jefferson gave birth to another baby girl, but the celebration was short-lived. Mrs. Jefferson was terribly ill following the birth, and she grew steadily worse over the summer. On September 6 she passed away. Martha was only thirty-four years old. Just when the dark clouds seemed to be lifting, Thomas Jefferson plummeted yet again into deep despair and painful anguish.

He remained in his room for three weeks. "When at last he left his room," his daughter Patsy remembered, "he rode out, and from that time he was incessantly on horseback, rambling about the mountain, in the least frequented roads, and just as often through the woods. In those melancholy ramblings I was his constant companion—a solitary witness to many a burst of grief."

Again he sought comfort in the wilderness he knew as a boy. He seemed to wander, his broken spirit trying desperately to find its way. "There is a time in human suffering," he wrote in his account book, "when exceeding sorrows are but like snow falling on an iceberg."

Only thirty-nine, Thomas Jefferson had already buried his father and mother, his best friend, Dabney Carr, two sisters, three children, and now his beloved wife. Two years later, the baby girl that Martha had recently delivered also died. Jefferson was now a widower with two little girls. He never remarried. *Grief, misery, suffering*—the words are not strong enough to describe what he experienced in the fall and winter of 1782. In a letter written a few weeks later he said,

> Before that event my scheme of life had been determined. I had folded myself in the arms of retirement, and rested all prospects of future happiness on domestic & literary objects. A single event wiped away all my plans and left me a blank which I had not the spirit to fill up.

Jefferson the Warrior: Some Final Thoughts

In this chapter we have been witnesses to some of the greatest challenges Thomas Jefferson ever encountered in his life. We have seen him endure humiliating public defeat, failure, and intense personal sorrow. We have watched him tumble into the pit of despair and bitterness. But as Jefferson's life would show, defeat is never an end for great leaders but merely the prologue to an as yet unwritten chapter of victory.

- People need to be reminded that they are important and that their contributions really do matter. It's the duty of a leader to make sure their actions are appreciated and their sacrifices make sense.
- When the going gets tough and you don't seem to be getting anywhere, ask yourself, What do I do best? What are my talents? Am I putting them to work to win this victory? Figure out how your talents can contribute to realizing the goals of your team, and put that plan into action without delay.
- Information is the greatest resource. Good leaders make

every effort to ensure that they have access to the most timely and reliable information possible.

- Even in times of profound struggle leaders do not forget the big picture. No matter how many battles have been lost, the war can still be won.
- Leadership can be terribly lonely and intensely frustrating. You may get criticism for failing when you were expecting praise for trying.
- Responsibility is not always convenient, nor is it easy. At times, being a leader will demand everything you've got, and then some. It will push you physically and emotionally, and force you to discover a fortitude you may not have known you possessed.
- Just because you have enjoyed past successes does not mean you are invincible. Unforeseen circumstances can appear to overwhelm you with incredible odds. How you respond at these times will determine what kind of a leader you really are. Adversity is the ultimate test of real leadership.
- Where is *your* Monticello? All leaders need a safe haven to which they can go to nourish their spirits and rest.
- In the face of defeat, throw yourself into work that you are good at and truly enjoy. This will renew your confidence and strength.

CHAPTER 6

JEFFERSON THE SLAVEHOLDER

The whole commerce between master and slave is a perpetual exercise of the most boisterous passions, the most unremitting despotism on the one part, and degrading submissions on the other.

In this chapter we will consider Thomas Jefferson's political maneuvers to combat the spread of slavery and his personal complicity in perpetuating it. How a man could argue so eloquently for liberty and justice yet refuse to take steps to end the abhorrent institution in his own home continues to be one of the great paradoxes in American history.

Rather than lose ourselves in this contentious debate, it is important to consider what this issue says about Jefferson's leadership. Is this the story of a man who tried earnestly to lead a fight against slavery but failed? Or did he simply refuse to offer leadership at all? In the end, the answer lies somewhere in the middle ground.

"HEAVEN WAS SILENT"

In October 1783, over a year after his wife's death, Jefferson left Monticello and dutifully accepted an appointment to Congress, which was then meeting in Annapolis, Maryland. He could have stayed at home, quietly attending to his farm, his "literary objects," and redesigning his house; his friends would have understood. But they urged him to return to public life. Jefferson accepted.

Exactly why he left the domestic life he had so vigorously committed himself to a year and a half before, we don't know. But it's a good bet that with his wife gone, the private life he had once longed for was no longer possible. "Home" never again meant the same thing to him after Martha died. And Jefferson spent the greater part of his remaining years in public service. The "arms of retirement" into which he had joyously folded himself had released him.

During his six months as a congressional delegate Jefferson rededicated himself to the behind-the-scenes committee work for which he was supremely qualified. Historian Wendell Garret noted that Jefferson "assumed a position of commanding leadership among all his colleagues. He was placed on every important committee, served as chairman of most of them, and wrote almost all of the important public papers to come out of this Congress."

He was responsible for establishing the base units of American currency—dollar, dime, and cent—oversaw the ratification of the peace treaty with England, and drafted the criteria by which new states would be admitted to the union. The latter legislation, which he submitted to Congress the following March, is known to history as the Ordinance of 1784. As Jefferson originally proposed the ordinance, it called for the end of slavery in all new states after the year 1800. But thanks to some fierce lobbying by Southern pro-slavery delegates, Congress chose to delete that clause from the ordinance—by one vote. Jefferson was most disappointed. He later recalled to a friend,

> The voice of a single individual of the state which was divided or of one of those which were of the negative would have

prevented this abominable crime from spreading itself over the new country. Thus we see the fate of millions unborn hanging on the tongue of one man, and Heaven was silent in that awful moment! But it is to be hoped it will not always be silent and that the friends to the rights of human nature will in the end prevail.

TROUBLING PARADOX

This was not the first time that Jefferson had spoken out against slavery or proposed legislation to bring it to an end. The Ordinance of 1784 is particularly important, however, as historian Joseph Ellis has written, because it was not only "the most far-reaching proposal to end slavery that Jefferson ever wrote but also the high-water mark of his antislavery efforts, which receded afterward to lower levels of caution and procrastination."

Up to this point in his life, Jefferson had been an advocate for the end of the slave trade and for emancipation of some kind. But beginning around this time he grew ever more quiet on the subject and increasingly reluctant to take on the cause. He consciously abdicated his leadership position on the issue, preferring instead to focus on other matters.

To make a fair assessment of Jeffersonian leadership, it's imperative that we consider his relationship to slavery—the way he felt about it, the way he dealt with it, and the ways he *didn't* deal with it. It's one of the most troubling conundrums of the American experience. How could the man who said "all men are created equal" and are entitled to "life, liberty, and the pursuit of happiness" have bought and sold other human beings?

How can a country that was founded on individual freedom simultaneously accept the miserable tyranny of slavery?

In his *Notes on the State of Virginia,* Thomas Jefferson wrote that civilization teaches us to "respect those rights in others which we value in ourselves." Though he obviously believed that on some level, he practiced the principle only to a point. It was certainly not the guiding premise at Monticello, where the natural rights of black men, women, and children to live free were systematically suppressed on a daily basis. How could Jefferson have continued to play a prominent role in such a dehumanizing institution? Where was his leadership when it was needed most?

"MY FAMILY"

When Thomas Jefferson wrote the Declaration of Independence in 1776, over half a million people in America, one fifth of the population, were enslaved. The African slave trade was a significant part of the national economy—important to business interests in the North as well as in the South. Jefferson had been partially raised by and had grown up with enslaved African Americans. In fact, his first memory as a child was of being carried on a pillow by a slave.

As a grown man he owned approximately 170 African-American individuals on his various estates. African Americans at Monticello worked Monday through Saturday, sunup to sundown, providing for every necessity and comfort that Jefferson and his family depended on. Employing a romanticism that disguised the actual horrors of slavery, Jefferson referred to the African Americans at Monticello as "my family"—a term widely used by Southern slaveowners at the time. He described enslaved people as "those who labor for my happiness."

In a way, slavery made sense to Jefferson. He considered African Americans "much inferior" to whites and thus declared that they needed to be taken care of. He wrote that letting "persons whose habits have been formed in slavery" go free would be like "abandoning children." Jefferson believed African Americans incapable of poetry or art for "in imagination they are dull, tasteless, and anomalous"—a view that prefigured the scientific racism of the 1800s. He also wrote that

> I advance it therefore as a suspicion only, that the blacks, whether originally a distinct race, or made distinct by time and circumstances, are inferior to the whites in the endowments both of body and mind. . . . This unfortunate difference of color, and perhaps of faculty, is a powerful obstacle to the emancipation of these people.

Jefferson seems to have believed that *owning* African Americans, in his experience at least, was akin to *caring* for them. To his way of thinking, the master–slave relationship had elements of affection. For that reason he purposefully distanced himself from the repulsive realities of slavery—the humiliation, the brutality, the whippings, the beatings, the destruction of families, the death of spirit—because these events challenged his paternalistic fantasies.

"TO TEMPORIZE"

On another level—at times political but more often philosophical—Thomas Jefferson was absolutely opposed to slavery, and he spoke out against it often in his writings. The institution of slavery was, in his words, "an abominable crime."

> The whole commerce between master and slave is a perpetual exercise of the most boisterous passions, the most unremitting despotism on the one part, and degrading submissions on the other.

As a lawmaker he sponsored various pieces of legislation aimed against slavery and the slave trade—some of which, like the statute to end the importation of slaves from Africa to Virginia, were successful. Most others, like the antislavery clause in the Ordinance of 1784, were not.

This is not to say that Thomas Jefferson advocated the complete and unqualified emancipation of slaves in America. Historian Paul Finkelman has written that even though Jefferson may have condemned slavery, "he was far more concerned about what slavery did to whites than about what it did to blacks. He was fearful of miscegenation, the enslavement of whites, and violent conflict between the races." Given the racism and fear that had been culturally engrained in him as a child—and which he had consciously chosen not to reject as an adult—he had no vision for a free black and white population enjoying the liberties of American life together.

"Nothing is more certainly written in the book of fate," Thomas Jefferson wrote, "than that these people are to be free. Nor is it less certain that the two races, equally free, cannot live in the same government." Historian Joseph Ellis observes that as a young man, Jefferson "assumed a leadership role in pushing slavery onto the agenda in the Virginia Assembly and the federal Congress" and that

> he was a member of the vanguard that insisted on the incompatibility of slavery with the principles on which the American republic was founded. Throughout this early phase of his life it would have been unfair to accuse him of hypocrisy for owning slaves or to berate him for failing to provide moral leadership on America's most sensitive political subject. It would in fact have been fairer to applaud his efforts, most of them admittedly futile, to inaugurate antislavery reform, and to

wonder admiringly how this product of Virginia's planter class had managed to develop such liberal convictions.

But as he grew older, certainly in the wake of the debate over his Ordinance of 1784 legislation, Thomas Jefferson came to believe that continuing to lead the political fight against slavery worked against his leadership on other issues. He came to a point in his life where he just didn't think the cause could be won. The opposition was simply too strong, he thought; besides, he had no real solutions for the problem anyway. Moreover, he reaped terrific financial benefits from the labor of enslaved African Americans at Monticello. He had a rhetorical vision for an end to slavery—but no plan for how it could actually be brought about, given his own prejudices and fears, and those of the majority of white Americans.

Somewhat similarly to a contemporary politician's approach to the emotionally polarizing issues we face today—abortion, for example—Jefferson determined slavery to be almost too hot to handle politically. He seemed to believe that it was, to put it bluntly, a bad career move to keep arguing the case against slavery. Historian and Jefferson interpreter Clay Jenkinson describes it like this:

> And so he learned a lesson. He realized that if he went to the wall as an absolutist on the issue of slavery that he would lose his credibility on other fronts that were equally important to him. And in a sense from the middle of his life he began to temporize and he began to talk about the next generation and he postponed slavery as America postponed the issue of slavery. And Jefferson is right at the heart of this national paradox.

"RECONCILE YOURSELF"

Beginning in the early 1780s, Jefferson—like countless politicians since—moved toward the blurry ideological center, where there was much less conflict and he was politically more comfortable. The result is that he no longer provided the leadership he had offered (limited though it had been) in the fight against slavery.

He did remain willing to speak out against the institution in his writings—safe in the lofty realm of words and ideas. And as president he introduced legislation that ended the importation of slaves into America—which, of course, did nothing for the African Americans already in chains or the generations of children that would be born into bondage.

In terms of being willing to go well beyond rhetoric and take up a personal lead against slavery in the United States, Jefferson proved that he could not provide the forwardness and zeal that the times required. In 1805 Jefferson commented that "I have long since given up the expectation of an early provision for the extinguishment of slavery among us."

He concluded that slavery would die a natural death or that a younger, bolder generation would take the lead and end it. "This enterprise is for the young," he wrote. But when younger slaveowners contacted him, telling him of their desires to free their slaves, Jefferson told them not to do it. As he responded to one of these young men in 1814,

> My opinion has ever been that, until more can be done for them, we should endeavor, with those whom fortune has

> thrown on our hands, to feed and clothe them well, protect them from all ill usage, require such reasonable labor only as is performed voluntarily by freemen, & be led by no repugnancies to abdicate them, and our duties to them. . . . I hope then, my dear sir, you will reconcile yourself to your country and its unfortunate condition.

In the end, despite the efforts he had at some points made to oppose slavery, Thomas Jefferson died a slaveholder. Over the course of his lifetime he freed less than ten of his slaves. The remaining 130 enslaved African Americans of his estate were sold after he died to help pay off his enormous debts. When push came to shove, Jefferson was unwilling to compromise his political clout and his personal comfort to combat this "abominable crime."

"THE BEST OF HIS GENERATION"

It is incorrect to believe that Jefferson did all he could do to combat slavery in America. There was actually a great deal more he *could* have done both publicly and privately—beginning, obviously, with freeing his own slaves. But he made a conscious decision as a politician not to do this. The legislative fight against slavery was a hot potato he was no longer willing to hold, so he passed it on. As a private slaveholder he opted to maintain the status quo and keep the vast majority of his slaves in bondage. Jefferson plainly elected to abdicate his leadership on the issue. And it is on this point that history has judged him most harshly.

It's important to understand that we are not holding Jefferson to our twenty-first-century standards of what is right and wrong. "Criticism of Jefferson," historian Paul Finkelman has written, "for his failure to act on slavery must be based on what his own generation expected from him and on comparing his actions with those of others in his generation." In a filmed interview Finkelman underscores that point:

> One of the defenses of Jefferson is always, well, he was just a Virginia planter, and we can't expect anything else from him. He's just like his neighbors. And I think the point to be made is that he was not like his neighbors. We don't build monuments to people who are just like their neighbors. We don't put them on the nickel. We don't make them icons. Jefferson was a very special man, and we can expect more from him. And so we compare him to the best of his generation. We compare him to George Washington who freed his slaves, to his cousin John Randolph of Roanoke who freed his slaves, to his neighbor Edward Coles, to the thousands of individual small Virginians who freed their slaves. The freed black population in Virginia grows from about two thousand to over thirty thousand in the space of about thirty years. A lot of Virginians are freeing their slaves. Where's the master of Monticello? Why isn't he there?

Thomas Jefferson must have been well aware that he was taking the low road on slavery, the easy way out. Progressives around the country and in Europe openly criticized him for not living up to the promise of his own words. But Jefferson simply wasn't up for the struggle or the conflict that an abolitionist's agenda would have brought him. As Finkelman concludes, "Jefferson was more concerned with avoiding irritation than promoting emancipation."

THE LEGACY

Though he was willing to risk his reputation, his wealth, his home, even his life in a struggle for freedom against England, Thomas Jefferson was not willing to do anything of the kind to secure the liberty of African Americans. Though he battled "narrow limits" of "habitual belief" in one arena, he was not willing to do so in another.

On no other issue does the legacy of Thomas Jefferson continue to generate more controversy. It is here that his sharpest critics still take aim in condemnation. Jefferson's lifelong experience with slavery—his paradoxical aversion to and acceptance of it—provides us with an opportunity to appreciate four very important lessons about leadership.

1. You Will Be Judged

Most people who will read this book will not have to worry about historians examining their every move. But all leaders—whether in politics, business, sports, the arts, education, or in the community—must be prepared for some degree of scrutiny. Family members, coworkers, teammates, students, and neighbors will be there. And they will all be watching.

That means that your actions and, even more important, your failure to act in some cases will not be missed. And if you choose to abdicate your leadership on a tough issue, to compromise your principles, your decision will most assuredly not go unnoticed by those around you. Be prepared for that ahead of time.

To what extent are you willing to stand on principle? to fight for what you believe in? to jeopardize your own comfort? to risk your reputation in the name of an unpopular cause that you believe is just? Effective leaders must be willing to sacrifice something for the rare ability they enjoy to influence the lives of others. Leadership doesn't come freely or easily. You will be judged. You will be tested. Your courage will be measured.

2. *Refuse to Abdicate Your Leadership*

Americans would love to be able to say that Thomas Jefferson went to his grave having done everything he could possibly have done to take a stand against the enslavement of human beings. But that just wasn't the case. That fact continues to mystify, disappoint, frustrate, and anger us. For a complex web of reasons, Jefferson abdicated the leadership against slavery that he had so boldly assumed as a young man. He surrendered the responsibility and walked away from the fight.

The fundamental lesson that we can draw from this today is never to abdicate your leadership. It's likely that every single person reading this book right now is facing an incredibly tough challenge or moral dilemma in life. Facing that problem head-on with the conviction of your principles to guide you demands leadership, tenacity, and nerve.

If there is one line to remember from this book, it is this: *Refuse to abdicate your leadership*. Once you've assumed the leadership role in your life, refuse to turn away from the most trying challenges when they confront you. Do not sacrifice your principles for comfort. Do not compromise your integrity for ease. Join the fight for what is right.

3. *Walk the Walk*

After Jefferson chose to no longer take the lead in the political fight against slavery, he retreated to the comfortable world of rhetoric. There, isolated from the conflict of public life, his words "softly but steadily" (as he once described it) spoke in opposition to the practice. But in his actions, Jefferson continued to actively support the practice of slavery on his own land. "The history of Jefferson's relationship to slavery is grim and unpleasant," Finkelman has written. "His words are those of a liberty-loving man of the Enlightenment. His deeds are those of a self-indulgent and negrophobic Virginia planter."

This poses a question every leader must finally answer: Do your deeds manifest your words? Do you walk the walk or just talk the talk? Do you support what you believe by what you say and what you do? Or is there a glaring disconnect between the two? Know this: People will be more willing to accept your vision and embrace your leadership if you walk the walk in your own life.

4. Prepare for Power

Whatever transgressions King George or the English parliament may have committed against the liberty of the colonists, they in no way matched the absolute horrors of slavery that were perpetuated by some of the same men who led the revolution. Motivated by a crude racism and a fear of the unknown, these men rationalized away the obvious contradictions in favor of habit and comfort.

Leadership offers power, and with power comes phenomenal responsibility. Historian Andrew Burstein has commented that Thomas Jefferson

> symbolizes the nation's tolerance for moral stagnation amid so much self-congratulation for its "progress." But it was never just Jefferson. It was everyone who belonged to the power structure. Power invites abuses and because it becomes comfortable, power produces widespread rationalizations for those abuses.

Aspiring leaders should prepare themselves for the responsibilities of power they will enjoy. At the same time, they should guard themselves against the abuses of that power and the "widespread rationalizations" that are often associated with it.

Jefferson the Slaveholder: Some Final Thoughts

In the preceding chapters we witnessed a leader who was willing to face tremendous adversity with courage and tenacity. We saw a man who risked everything to stand for a cause he truly believed in. In this chapter we saw the same man walk away from leadership, unwilling to manifest that same fearlessness in a tough fight in another worthy cause.

Like any leader, Jefferson had to pick his battles. As a young man he boldly chose to join the political assault on slavery. He assumed leadership and was the very person who might have had the convictions and political skills to wage a formidable attack on slavery in America. But he was compromised by his own prejudices and fears. He abdicated that leadership and retreated.

Many of his contemporaries and numerous Americans since have condemned Jefferson for that move. Many others have concluded that he did all he could do given the times in which he lived. But despite the debate over his legacy, there will always be much to learn from Thomas Jefferson—whether he is impressing us with his brilliance or disappointing us with his failures.

- Be willing to sacrifice. Leadership doesn't come freely or easily.
- Assuming a leadership role means that you will be judged; you will be tested. Your courage will be measured. Meet that challenge.
- Refuse to abdicate your leadership.
- Leaders are often required to stand on their principles—so protect them. Do not compromise your integrity for ease or comfort.
- What criteria do you use to pick your battles as a leader?

Do you pick the fights you think you can win or the ones that should be fought regardless of the chances of victory?

- Walk the walk—it's that simple. You weaken your position as a leader when your actions don't match your words.
- Be wary of rationalizations that mask the abuse of power. They can discredit your leadership and damage your legacy.

CHAPTER 7

JEFFERSON THE DIPLOMAT

I hold it that a little rebellion now and then is a good thing.

At various times throughout our lives each of us is called upon to serve as a diplomat—to represent our country, our families, our companies, our professions, our teams, our schools, or any of a variety of organizations to which we belong. Jefferson's five years representing the United States serve as a rich example of successful diplomacy that we might emulate.

Jefferson traveled to France in 1784, overseeing America's diplomatic efforts in Europe until 1789. After a bitter period in Virginia, both personally and publicly, the dramatic change of scenery and duty proved to be quite therapeutic. Jefferson excelled as a diplomat, relying on talents he had developed as a student in Williamsburg and as a Virginia politician. His accomplishments as a negotiator of trade treaties were nothing short of brilliant. Jefferson was well liked by his French counterparts and was often consulted by the leaders of the French Revolution—a momentous and bloody event that he witnessed first hand.

While Jefferson was serving in France the United States experienced a rebellion of its own. Former militia captain Daniel Shays, unhappy with new tax laws, led a revolt in Massachusetts in 1787. It was just one of many such disturbances around the country at this time. Jefferson responded positively to the news of Shays' Rebellion, describing it as a "medicine necessary for the sound health of government." The revolt expressed freedom among the citizenry and the opportunity of growth for the Union, an enormously promising sign to Jefferson.

AN AMERICAN IN PARIS

In the early morning hours of July 5, 1784, Jefferson set sail from Boston for Europe. He was accompanied by his eldest daughter, Patsy, not quite twelve. They enjoyed a smooth trip and beautiful weather. Patsy later recalled that the sea was "calm as a river." After some stops along the way, they arrived in Paris on August 6. Thomas Jefferson was forty-one years old and at the very start of a new chapter in his life.

Congress had chosen him to join John Adams and Benjamin Franklin to negotiate trade treaties and diplomatic ties with the nations of Europe. He enrolled Patsy in a French school and took up residence in an extravagant house near the present-day site of the Arch of Triumph. His French was never all that good, so he relied on interpreters throughout his stay.

Jefferson was appalled by the stark disparity inherent in the monarchical French society. The wealthy, well-fed, well-educated few ruled the country and enjoyed all it had to offer, while the mass of citizens lived in abject poverty, being illiterate, overworked, and undernourished. The experience made a profound impression on him that lasted for the rest of his life. The inequities of the traditional European societies reinforced his conviction that America should, by its own example, lead the world in a more humane and enlightened direction. He wrote home to a friend:

> Behold me at length on the vaunted scene of Europe! You are, perhaps, curious to know how this new scene has struck a

> savage of the mountains of America. Not advantageously, I assure you. I find the general fate of humanity here most deplorable. The truth of Voltaire's observation offers itself perpetually, that every man here must be either the hammer or the anvil.

But at the same time, Thomas Jefferson was captivated by the glitz and glamour of the Parisian life to which he, as a visiting diplomat, had access. Though it was always on the periphery of his experience while in Europe, his was not the Paris of poverty and despair but that of elegant salons, dinner parties, and art galleries. A man of the Enlightenment who hungered for every opportunity to tantalize his senses with art and high culture, Jefferson was captivated with the French capital. He soon adopted France as a second home, and it always held a special place in his heart. Historian Clay Jenkinson observes in an interview that

> suddenly he was lowered as if from a hot air balloon into the glittering world of late aristocratic France. And it overwhelmed him. He was intoxicated by its beauty and its decadence and its intrigue, its flirtation, its architecture, its music, its dance, its literature, its science. He knew he shouldn't love it. But he was overwhelmed by it. And it was an awakening for Jefferson.

ACCEPT THE CALL TO ADVENTURE

One of the fundamental reasons Jefferson went to France was to move beyond pain. Had he stayed at home he would constantly have been reminded of his heartbreaking loss. Though he always loved Monticello, following Martha's death it was an environment steeped in sadness, and he knew he needed some distance from it to recover. On another level, the diplomatic mission to Paris was a great excuse to see Europe. And it provided him with a chance to reinvigorate his career as well as to get beyond the rumors of incompetence that still tainted his tenure as governor. He enthusiastically seized the opportunity.

Like Jefferson, any leader is willing to face new challenges, recognizing in them the possibilities to renew purpose, reawaken strength, and achieve greater goals. To do this a leader must not be afraid to leave his or her comfort zone and travel to unfamiliar territory. Take advantage of the change of scenery, the new circumstances, and the fresh faces.

Accept the call to adventure, and see in the journey an opening to grow as a person and to reinvent or redefine your leadership.

"C'EST VOUS?"

One of the first significant challenges that Jefferson faced in France was, of all things, a promotion. When Benjamin Franklin resigned from his post and returned to the United States in 1785, Congress appointed Jefferson to succeed him. At about the same time the Congress sent John Adams to London as minister to Great Britain, which left Jefferson at the helm of the entire diplomatic mission in the heart of Europe. After only a few months, he had found himself almost single-handedly in charge of America's foreign relations.

But following on the heels of the charming, affable Franklin was no easy task. Franklin had achieved celebrity status in Europe, and the French greatly lamented his departure. Jefferson noted, "There appeared to me more respect and veneration attached to the character of Dr. Franklin in France than to that of any other person in the same country, foreign or native." Because they were so disappointed to see Franklin go, the French didn't exactly welcome Jefferson with open arms. The way many of them saw it, the larger-than-life Benjamin Franklin had been replaced with a reserved, quiet, and somewhat stiff Virginian. It was a difficult position for Jefferson to be in, as it would have been for anyone who followed Franklin. Jefferson later wrote that

> the succession to Dr. Franklin at the court of France was an excellent school of humility. On being presented to anyone as the minister of America, the commonplace question used in such cases was "C'est vous, Monsieur, qui remplace le Docteur Franklin?"—"Is it you, sir, who replace Dr. Franklin?" I generally answered "No one can replace him, sir; I am only his successor."

SCHOOL OF HUMILITY

It's never easy being someone's successor, especially when that person has achieved a great deal and has won the admiration and praise of others. But all leaders at one time or another will eventually find themselves enrolled in just such a "school of humility."

You will hear stories repeated again and again about how wonderful your predecessor was—just as Jefferson did about Franklin. And people will be quick to remind you how your predecessor did things and what made him or her so incredibly effective. People will seem eager to compare you to whoever came before. You will find yourself in someone else's shadow, which is not a particularly comfortable place for any leader to be. But it will happen; when it does, take a cue from Thomas Jefferson.

First, whatever you do, refrain from discrediting the memory of whoever preceded you. Far from empowering you, such comments or actions will make you appear petty and will undermine your leadership. Instead, join others in their appreciation for the character and accomplishments of your predecessor. Humble yourself to their legacy and recognize that by doing so, you bolster the office or position you now hold—and, in turn, your own prospects as a leader.

Second, don't focus your efforts on overcoming the shadow of your predecessor. Strive rather to cast your own shadow, and to build a unique legacy and reputation on your own terms. Leaders never reach the point where they cease having to prove themselves. That's just one of many qualities that makes leadership and success in any field so demanding. The great leaders are those who are ever willing to meet that challenge and take classes in the "school of humility."

NEGOTIATION AND DIPLOMACY

Over the next few years, Thomas Jefferson won the respect and admiration of many in France even though his diplomatic style was not nearly as outgoing and engaging as Franklin's had been. Just how did he do it? He demonstrated seven key themes of quality negotiation and diplomacy.

1. Employ a Balanced, Steady Pressure . . .

Jefferson's goal as a negotiator of new trade treaties in Europe was to help American merchants—who had hitherto relied almost solely on Great Britain—develop positive new relationships on the international scene. He dealt primarily with the commerce of whale oils, fish, meat, rice, and tobacco. And he enjoyed some success with Prussia, Denmark, Italy, and France. As an advocate of free trade among nations, Jefferson diligently worked against the price-fixing of

French aristocrats and the entrenched old-world monopolies that had a chokehold on international trade. Historian Wendell Garrett writes that

> Jefferson finally achieved his purpose, indirectly and very effectively through a steady pressure. . . . In his obstinate and patient endeavor to obtain for the United States commercial rights, and even privileges, that would enable her to pay off her debts to European bankers, Jefferson was earnest but prudent, candid but careful not to offend, with a balanced sense of his diplomatic position which prevented zeal from overtaking discretion. . . . Through sheer persistence and hard work, he had saved the credit and honor of his country. . . . [Jefferson] played a brilliant part in laying the foundation of this new nation's international policy and set for the future the highest standard of dignified diplomacy.

Talk about casting your own shadow!

2. *But Don't Press Those Who Aren't Ready*

Thomas Jefferson remembered that while some countries were ready and willing to negotiate new treaties, some others were not.

> Other powers appearing indifferent, we did not think it proper to press them. They seemed, in fact, to know little about us but as rebels who had been successful in throwing off the yoke of the mother country. They were ignorant of our commerce, which had been always monopolized by England, and of the exchange of articles it might offer advantageously to both parties. They were inclined, therefore, to stand aloof until they could see better what relations might be usefully instituted with us.

Part of maintaining that important delicate balance is realizing that not everyone will be ready or eager to negotiate with you. Be patient. It's okay to let others "stand aloof" and watch until they can "see better." Don't "press them." They want to see what you have to offer first and watch you work with other parties before they join in. Initiate deals and programs where you can, and use them as examples to entice others.

3. *Take Advantage of Well-placed Allies*

Jefferson's proverbial ace-in-the-hole during his negotiations with the French was the former Revolutionary War hero, the French general Marquis de Lafayette, who had assisted Washington at Yorktown. Beginning in 1785, Jefferson and Lafayette began a warm friendship that lasted into their old age.

Their mutual admiration, combined with Lafayette's connections to powerful players in the French government, led to many successful treaties that benefited both countries. As a diplomat, Jefferson declared that he was "powerfully aided" by Lafayette and held him in especially high regard for all he had done for America.

In all your negotiations seek to cultivate well-placed allies who can advise you and skillfully represent your position. And remember, it's not always who you know—it's who *they* know.

4. *Negotiate from Strength*

Despite his aversion to war, Thomas Jefferson understood military strength as a critical factor in dealing with other countries. In a 1785 letter to American statesman John Jay, Jefferson made this point clear. "Weakness provokes insult and injury," he wrote, "while a condition to punish it often prevents it. This reasoning leads to the necessity of some naval force, that being the only weapon with which we can reach an enemy. I think it to our interest to punish the first insult, because an insult unpunished is the parent of many others. We are not at this moment in a condition to do it, but we should put ourselves into it as soon as possible."

Every leader should appreciate the principle of negotiating from strength. You don't have to have your own naval force, however, to express a strength of purpose, character, and vision. And remember that often the best way to "punish the first insult" is with your own success.

5. Build a Coalition

While he was in Europe Jefferson had to deal with the terrorist actions of Barbary pirates from the north coast of Africa. For years these militant pirates had seized foreign ships, stolen goods, and taken hostages. In the mid 1780s the terrorists demanded a cash ransom for some American hostages, and Jefferson was one of the point men overseeing the negotiations for the United States. Jefferson was firmly opposed to giving in to the terrorists' demands. If you give in to blackmail once, he reasoned, then the terrorists will never stop taking advantage of you; as he put it, "an insult unpunished is the parent of many others."

Jefferson had another tactic in mind. In 1786 he suggested that the United States build a coalition of nations to oppose terrorism—a brilliant strategy, even by today's standards. But Congress dragged its feet when it came to committing its share of the necessary finances, and the plan fell apart. The freedom of the American hostages was eventually bought for $30,000—and just as Jefferson predicted, the terrorist attacks continued.

Jefferson's idea was certainly well ahead of its time. Hard to believe, but in the late eighteenth century he proposed what we might think of today as a United Nations peacekeeping force. It would be left to future generations to discover the wisdom of his vision.

6. Develop Personal Relationships

During his stay in France, Jefferson regularly hosted lavish dinner parties and entertained French nobles at his home. He developed personal relationships that served him quite well in his public role as a negotiator of treaties. Jefferson learned that a dinner party could be much more than just good food, fine wine, beautiful music, and pleasant conversation. It could be a diplomatic event that laid the groundwork for successful agreements. It's a principle that diplomats have often followed. And years later as president, Jefferson cleverly put that same tactic to work in the White House. Don't underestimate the power of personal relationships. Such associations are often at the core of successful political and business ventures.

7. Be a Better Listener Than You Are a Talker

One of the greatest mistakes that negotiators make is to talk too much. They believe that by explaining themselves or their position in greater detail, they will secure the objectives they are aiming for. Just the opposite is often true. There is a time to talk, no doubt. But quite often the best negotiating tactic is simply to keep your mouth shut and listen. Empathize. Embody patience and courtesy. Nod your head. Make eye contact. Be understanding.

Ever the polite and patient diplomat, Thomas Jefferson made superb use of this principle during his time in France. (It was an approach made all the easier, it should be pointed out, by the fact that he usually relied on interpreters.) Active listening was a skill he had learned well sitting at Governor Fauquier's table as a young college student, keenly soaking up his mentors' debates on philosophy and science. Listening, for Jefferson, was a part of the learning process with which he was infinitely comfortable. He was never one to monopolize a conversation, often preferring to sit back and hear what others had to say. It is a valuable talent and one that leaders should strive to cultivate.

"HEAD AND HEART"

Thomas Jefferson's years in Paris are not only memorable for his demonstrations of superb diplomacy. In 1786 Jefferson traveled to London, where he and John Adams attempted unsuccessfully to arrange trade treaties with Great Britain. At one point on the trip, when Jefferson and Adams were presented to George III, the king ceremoniously turned his back on the two Americans. Years later in his autobiography, Jefferson recalled this incident with the king, blasting the "ulcerations in the narrow mind of that mulish being."

Back in Paris that summer, Jefferson met the beautiful, twenty-seven-year-old Maria Cosway, the wife of an English painter then visiting France. She flirted with the forty-three-year-old Jefferson, who responded in kind. Their painfully brief, romantic affair—which has since attained an almost mythic status—lasted through the late summer and autumn of 1786.

When Cosway finally departed Paris with her husband in October, the sentimental Jefferson was devastated. He wrote that he felt "more dead than alive." He summed up his conflicting emotions for her in a moving and now famous letter, "Dialogue Between My Head and My Heart." Cosway made no attempt to rekindle the affair and barely responded to Jefferson's long letter.

TROUBLE AT HOME

While Jefferson mended his broken heart in Paris, the United States was dealing with an outbreak of violence. In the wake of the Revolutionary War, the nation was hit by an economic depression as a result of ruined trade relations with Britain. In rural New England especially, working-class farmers bore the brunt of the dismal economy. Many of them were veterans of the war and had left their farms and risked their lives for independence. But most went uncompensated for their sacrifices. Thousands of them came home from the battlefields with near-worthless I.O.U.s from a money-strapped Congress, only to face the likelihood of debtor's prison.

As the economic situation worsened, state taxes spiraled out of control. Farmers and poorer citizens watched as the courts seized and liquidated their property—most of the money going to compensate lawyers and to pay wealthy creditors and big business interests in places like Boston. Each time the courts convened, more citizens lost their homes and their freedom. Many farmers began to voice the complaint that the revolution had done little but supplant a British ruling class with an American one.

Frustrated by a runaway economy that appeared to favor the wealthy few at the expense of everyone else, and disenchanted by an unresponsive government, thousands of farmers across New England took matters into their own hands. In a series of armed revolts throughout 1786 they prevented courts from convening and demanded redress of their grievances. Their leader was a thirty-nine-year-old Massachusetts farmer and former Revolutionary War captain named Daniel Shays.

Shays' Rebellion, as the uprising would come to be known, came to an end during the last week of January 1787. Attempting to capture an arsenal of weapons in Springfield, Massachusetts, Shays and roughly two thousand farmers were soundly defeated by the state militia and sent scattering into the countryside. Shays and thirteen others were subsequently sentenced to hang for their part in the rebellion. They were later pardoned, however, in a symbolic gesture of conciliation by Massachusetts governor John Hancock.

"LIBERTY ENOUGH"

News of Shays' Rebellion spread rapidly through Europe. Many of Jefferson's aristocratic American friends—who identified more with the elite creditors, lawyers, and judges than they did the struggling farmers—thought the armed resistance was nothing less than treason.

Abigail Adams denounced the rebels as "ignorant, restless desperadoes, without conscience or principles [who] have led a deluded multitude to follow their standard, under pretence of grievances which have no existence but in their imaginations." When he learned of the rebellion, George Washington said that he was "mortified beyond expression" and that the uprising was "a triumph for the advocates of despotism." Chief Justice William Cushing described Shays and his men as "ignorant, unprincipled, bankrupt, desperate individuals."

Thomas Jefferson was almost alone among U.S. leaders at the time who was not alarmed by Shays' Rebellion. On the contrary, his reaction was generally positive. In a series of letters written in the months following the revolts, Jefferson produced some of the most inspiring observations about liberty that ever came from his pen. His reaction to the rebellion is a lesson in tolerance and prudence that every leader would do well to study. In a letter to Ezra Stiles of Yale College Jefferson wrote,

> The commotions which have taken place in America, as far as they are yet known to me, offer nothing threatening. They are a proof that the people have liberty enough, and I would not wish them less than they have. If the happiness of the mass of the people can be secured at the expense of a little tempest now and then, or even of a little blood, it will be a precious purchase.

In an often-quoted letter to James Madison, Jefferson declared,

> I hold it that a little rebellion now and then is a good thing, and as necessary in the political world as storms in the physical. . . . It is a medicine necessary for the sound health of government. . . . Educate and inform the whole mass of the people. Enable them to see that it is their interest to preserve peace and order, and they will preserve them. . . . They are the only sure reliance for the preservation of our liberty.

To Abigail Adams Jefferson wrote that the "spirit of resistance to government is so valuable on certain occasions, that I wish it to be always kept alive." And in perhaps his most famous comment concerning the insurgence, Jefferson remarked to John Adams' son-in-law, William Smith,

> God forbid we should ever be twenty years without such a rebellion. . . . The tree of liberty must be refreshed from time to time with the blood of patriots & tyrants. It is its natural manure.

TOLERATE DISSENT

Thomas Jefferson displayed a judicious calm in response to Shays' Rebellion. Being in Paris, far removed from the scene of conflict, made it possible to respond with more perspective and forethought. He was willing to try to understand the motivation behind the sometimes violent actions of the rebels. And he was genuinely pleased when they were pardoned. Jefferson understood that liberty has a price. Free citizens would—and should—take to the streets to make known their concerns. If domestic tranquility was upset in the process, so be it. The health of our liberty absolutely demands that people be willing to speak out and take a stand for their beliefs. That means that leaders should encourage an open, tolerant environment so that people are comfortable coming forward with their grievances and opinions.

The most important leadership principle Jefferson demonstrated in this episode is a simple one, yet it is one of the hardest for most leaders to practice. He refused to overreact. He kept his cool. When others were predicting civil war and the end of the American experiment in democracy, Thomas Jefferson was unruffled. He turned the events of 1786–87 on their head, and saw them as a positive sign of freedom. For Jefferson, Shays' Rebellion was not an omen of the end of democracy but proof that the United States was doing something right.

When faced with discontent, leaders are often well advised to view the situation in a positive light, as an indication that those involved care deeply about the issues at hand. Conflict can be a sign of vigor and a stimulus to growth. Remain composed, and assess the benefits that can come from dissent.

"AN ASSEMBLY OF DEMI-GODS"

Thomas Jefferson enjoyed a relaxing three-month tour of southern Europe in the summer of 1787. After he returned to Paris he received a copy of the draft of the United States Constitution, which had just been issued by the Constitutional Convention in Philadelphia and sent to the states for ratification.

Some of the greatest minds of the revolution were present at that convention—George Washington, Benjamin Franklin, Alexander Hamilton, Roger Sherman, George Mason, George Wythe, and Jefferson's young protégé, James Madison, who emerged as a brilliant leader in his own right. Jefferson referred to the convention as "an assembly of demi-gods." Had he not been on the diplomatic mission in Europe, Thomas Jefferson would surely have been counted among them. It is one of the great "what ifs?" of history to wonder how his presence might have affected the Constitutional Convention of 1787.

The heated debates, secretive meetings, and hard-fought compromises that produced the Constitution make for one of the most fascinating episodes in American history. Constitutional delegates grappled with tough questions that continue to be debated to this day: How strong should the federal government be? What should be its role? And what should be its relation to the state governments?

Many of those present in Philadelphia that summer believed that the national Congress previously formed under the Articles of Confederation was too weak and ineffective, and that it relied too much on the charity of the states. Events like Shays' Rebellion—which some elite delegates feared could easily have mushroomed into a nationwide revolt of farmers and the poor—were among the reasons cited for a strong central government to maintain order.

Jefferson objected to that logic. "The late rebellion in Massachusetts has given more alarm than I think it should have done," he wrote. "Nor will any degree of power in the hands of government prevent insurrections." But those representatives who argued for a powerful federal presence won the day. After four months of haggling behind closed doors, the delegates agreed on a Constitution that valued a separation of powers among three branches of government, each with its own checks and balances. The formula also included a two-part legislature with proportional representation in one body (the House of Representatives) and equal representation in another (the Senate). The plan was approved by a majority of the states the following year, and the U.S. Constitution became the law of the land.

"A BITTER PILL OR TWO"

Jefferson's reaction to the Constitution was mixed. While there was much he liked about the plan—an independent federal government and the separation of powers, for example—there were some things that really troubled him. "As to the Constitution," Jefferson wrote, "I find myself nearly a neutral. There is a great mass of good in it, in a very desirable form; but there is also to me a bitter pill or two."

Historian Wendell Garrett writes that Jefferson "knew full well that a republican form of government was quite compatible with oppression, and he held with vehemence to the principle that the individual citizen is entitled to protection against misrule and intolerance. He believed that human liberties were at least as important as property rights." What concerned Jefferson the most, then, was the fact that the Constitution failed to enumerate those liberties that citizens would enjoy in the United States. He pointed this out in a letter to James Madison shortly before Christmas, 1787.

> I will now add what I do not like. First, the omission of a bill of rights providing clearly and without the aid of sophisms for freedom of religion, freedom of the press, protection against standing armies, restriction against monopolies, the eternal and unremitting force of the habeas corpus laws, and trials by jury. . . . Let me add that a bill of rights is what the people are entitled to against every government on earth, general or particular, & what no just government should refuse, or rest on inferences.

Thanks to some deal-making and compromises among politicians, the first ten amendments to the Constitution, the "Bill of Rights," were proposed a couple of years later, and ratified by a majority of the states in 1791.

Jefferson had also objected to the fact that the Constitution failed to include term limits for elected offices, especially for the presidency. His fear was that the president would become "an officer for life" and thus re-create the fixed monarchies and hereditary positions of power that had corrupted the nations of Europe. The solution, as he saw it, was to limit the time that leaders could serve in those positions. Jefferson's wisdom was again well ahead of its time. It was not until 1951—more than 160 years later—that America limited the time a president could serve to two terms.

PLAY THE ROLE OF DIRECTOR

As a leader, Jefferson was nowhere near center stage in the creation of the U.S. Constitution. But he was not extremely out of the loop. Even though he was not physically present at the historic gathering that summer, his influence was definitely felt. His inspirational Declaration of Independence set the foundation upon which the Constitution was built. And convention delegates stayed in touch with him regarding the goings-on.

Prior to the meetings he had shipped hundreds of books to James Madison, which his protégé used to prepare himself for the meetings. Then, following the convention, Jefferson became one of the most vocal proponents for a Bill of Rights, which was adopted a few years later. This process of writing the Constitution and amending a Bill of Rights reminds us that leaders may not always be at the center of the action. But they can wield influence on events through the people who are.

Being the focal point of the action at center stage should not always be the goal of leaders. Sometimes they can effectively influence the action onstage through their work as a "director" behind the scenes.

Even with the "bitter pill or two," Jefferson warmed to the Constitution over time. He later referred to the document as "a good canvas on which some strokes only want retouching," and hailed the Convention of 1787 that produced it. "The example of changing a constitution by assembling the wise men of the state, instead of assembling armies, will be worth as much to the world as former examples we have given them. The Constitution . . . is unquestionably the wisest ever yet presented to men."

THE FRENCH REVOLUTION

Before he left Paris and returned to America in the fall of 1789, Thomas Jefferson watched as the French Revolution exploded into violence. He noted that the "American war seems first to have awakened the thinking part of this nation in general from the sleep of despotism in which they were sunk."

And awake they did. The representative body of the French people, known as the Third Estate, withdrew from the general congress and rechristened itself the National Assembly in June 1789. When the king attempted to crack down on them by having them locked out of their meeting hall, the delegates gathered in an indoor tennis court and resolved (the now famous "Tennis Court Oath") to stay committed to their cause until the rights of all French citizens were safeguarded in a new constitution. On July 14, 1789, revolutionaries stormed the massive

Bastille in Paris, which was then used as a prison and arsenal. Their victory symbolized the end of the monarchy and birth of civil liberties in France.

Throughout the process the ambassador from America was a trusted advisor to many of the men who led the revolution—some of whom, like Lafayette, had become his good friends. The visionary mind and pragmatic leadership of Thomas Jefferson were thus at work behind the scenes of the two great revolutions of the eighteenth century.

"I was much acquainted with the leading patriots of the assembly," Jefferson recalled. "Being from a country which had successfully passed through a similar reformation, they were disposed to my acquaintance and had some confidence in me. I urged most strenuously an immediate compromise; to secure what the government was now ready to yield, and trust to future occasions for what might still be wanting."

Despite his counsel for caution and compromise, the French Revolution spiraled out of control, split into factions, and grew even more violent. Four years later, in 1793, King Louis XVI and Queen Marie Antoinette were executed. A counterrevolution ensued, leading to the military dictatorship of a celebrated young general, Napoleon Bonaparte.

Jefferson the Diplomat: Some Final Thoughts

Along with his young daughters and two enslaved African Americans, John and Sally Hemings, whom he had brought from Monticello, Thomas Jefferson set sail for the United States in late October. He had really fallen in love with France, its people and its culture. The experience was good for his spirit and helped to renew his leadership. But he had been gone from home for five years, and it was time to return.

"A more benevolent people I have never known," he wrote of the French. "Their kindness and accommodation to strangers is unparalleled, and the hospitality of Paris is beyond anything I had conceived to be practicable in a large city." But "I am savage enough to prefer the woods, the wilds, and the independence of Monticello to all the brilliant pleasures of this gay capital." In spite of his wishes, Jefferson never saw Paris after that. In fact, he never left America again. Destiny had other things in mind for him.

- Leaders are willing to rise to new challenges, for they recognize in them the opportunity to renew purpose, reawaken strength, and achieve greater goals.
- Leaders are not afraid of leaving their comfort zones to challenge themselves in unfamiliar territory. Accept the call to adventure.
- Join others in appreciating the legacy of great leaders who have preceded you. Cast your own shadow, and be willing to enroll as a student in the "school of humility."
- Successful leaders apply the steady-pressure approach to negotiating: Be "earnest but prudent, candid but careful not to offend." Be persistent, but be willing to let others watch from the sidelines until they are ready to work with you.
- Take advantage of well-placed allies who can represent you and help fight for your cause.
- Negotiate from strength of purpose, character, and vision. And remember that the easiest way to "punish the first insult" is by the success of actions based on well-defined convictions.
- Effective leaders build a coalition of resources that advances their agenda in a win-win scenario for all involved.
- Have the patience and sincerity to establish positive personal relationships during your negotiations.

- Practice listening. Strive to be as good (or better) a listener as you are a talker.
- Leaders encourage an open, tolerant environment in which people feel comfortable coming forward with their grievances and opinions.
- Refuse to overreact. Keep your cool. Embody perspective and forethought.
- Assess the benefits that often come from dissent.
- Leaders can't always be at the center of the action. But they can wield influence on events through the people who are. Learn to use well-timed cues to impact the actions of others.

CHAPTER 8

JEFFERSON THE STATESMAN

The spirit of 1776 is not dead.

When Thomas Jefferson sailed back into Norfolk in late November 1789 the United States was a country of nearly four million people. Philadelphia was the largest city, and Jefferson's native Virginia was the most populous state. Nine out of ten Americans were involved in farming. After much public debate the new constitution had already been ratified by twelve of the thirteen states (Rhode Island came on board in May 1790). George Washington had been inaugurated as the country's first president in the spring of 1789 and was busy setting up his government in New York City, which was then the nation's capital.

Jefferson came home for what he thought would be a brief visit before returning to his post in Paris. But even before he reached Monticello he received a letter that dramatically altered his plans. That one letter would change not only the direction of his life but the future of the country he had helped to create. It also opened the door to the next and greatest period in the evolution of his leadership.

In the American Revolution of 1776 Thomas Jefferson had been a behind-the-scenes leader. He did his best work and was most effective as a member of legislative committees or alone in his room writing important documents like the Declaration of Independence or the Virginia Statute for Religious Freedom.

He was not a man who gave commanding, inspirational speeches. He was not a great debater. He was reserved and subtle; at the same time, he could be crafty and scheming.

By and large, Jefferson was not an executive leader like Washington or Patrick Henry. And when he had tried to be, as governor of Virginia, the circumstances had not worked in his favor.

That was about to change. During his years as the country's first secretary of state and as vice president to John Adams, the most critical decade 1789–99, Jefferson became the influential, executive leader of a counterrevolution that changed the future course of America and the world.

SERVICE TO A GREATER CAUSE

On his way back to Monticello, in December 1789, a messenger delivering a letter from the new president, George Washington, met Jefferson. While still in France, he had been appointed to serve as the nation's first secretary of state—a position that had only recently been created—and Washington was writing to find out if he would accept the position.

Jefferson later wrote that he received that letter "with real regret. My wish had been to return to Paris . . . and to see the end of the Revolution, which I then thought would be certainly and happily closed in less than a year. I then meant to return home, to withdraw from political life . . . to sink into the bosom of my family and friends and to devote myself to studies more congenial to my mind."

Jefferson expressed his reluctance in a written response to Washington, but left the final decision up to the President. To the benefit of all Americans since, Washington urged Jefferson to take the job and join him in New York. Jefferson remarked to his personal secretary, William Short, that "it is impossible to give a flat refusal to such a nomination." After a couple of months at Monticello, during which he hosted the wedding of his eldest daughter, Patsy, Jefferson rode to New York City in the spring of 1790. He was forty-six years old.

Once again Thomas Jefferson embodied a central tenet of great leadership. Though he was reluctant to accept the new assignment and would have preferred to do other things, he answered the call of duty.

Successful leaders have an instinctive sense of duty. It shapes their beliefs, their actions, and their character. An appreciation of duty and responsibility is at the very core of who they are.

"I WAS ASTONISHED"

New York was a city of only thirty-three thousand people when Jefferson arrived in March 1790. President Washington's residence and office were located in a mansion on "the Broadway." The secretary of state's office with its nine employees was located nearby. The seat of national government remained in New York for another few months before relocating to Philadelphia later in the year.

Jefferson was familiar with his fellow leaders in President Washington's cabinet. His old friend John Adams was vice president; Henry Knox headed up the War Department; Virginian Edmund Randolph was attorney general; and Alexander Hamilton, one of Washington's young protégés, who had served with him during the war, was the first secretary of the Treasury.

Jefferson's friend and ally, James Madison, represented Virginia in the House of Representatives. Madison had worked very closely as an advisor to Washington in setting up the new government; along with Hamilton and John Jay, Madison had written the *Federalist Papers,* a series of editorials in New York newspapers that argued in favor of the new constitution. But recently Madison had become alarmed by what was going on behind the scenes, and he was especially concerned with how much power Hamilton had assumed.

Madison was particularly unnerved when the Senate resolved that Washington's official title would be "His Highness the President of the United States and Protector of their Liberties." Thanks to Madison and the delegates in the House, that title was changed to the simpler "President of the United States." In a letter to Jefferson, Madison shared his concerns that the government was "in a wilderness without a single footstep to guide us." He was relieved when his mentor left Monticello and headed for New York.

It didn't take long for Jefferson to see what was going on, and he too grew concerned. Things had changed greatly in the five years he had been away. Historian Wendell Garrett writes that Jefferson sensed "a kind of weariness and cynicism" and was disheartened to see that "the tyrannical system of England was now admired and emulated, while the rising revolutionary spirit of France was feared and dreaded." Jefferson wrote,

> When I arrived at New York in seventeen hundred and ninety to take a part in the administration, being fresh from the French Revolution while in its first and pure stage, and consequently somewhat whetted up in my own republican principles, I found a state of things which I could not have supposed possible. I was astonished to find the general presence of monarchical sentiments.

"THE RICH AND THE WELL-BORN"

Nowhere perhaps were those sentiments more apparent than in the office of the secretary of the Treasury. Thirty-three-year-old Alexander Hamilton—brilliant, brash, and extremely ambitious—was not shy about expressing his vision for an energetic federal government. As he saw it, one of the essential purposes of government was to safeguard and promote the interests of the wealthy few—they were, after all, the people who mattered most. Hamilton once wrote that

> all communities divide themselves into the few and the many. The first are the rich and the well-born, the other are the mass of the people. The voice of the people has been said to be the voice of God; and however generally this maxim has been quoted and believed, it is not true in fact. The people are turbulent and changing; they seldom judge or determine right. Give therefore to the first class a distinct permanent share in the government. . . . Nothing but a permanent body can check the imprudence of democracy.

For Hamilton, democracy was a "poison" and a "disease" that would destroy any hope of prosperity for the United States. He felt that the will of the people was untrustworthy, and that the new country was better left to the guidance of a small monied class. Hamilton saw a strong federal government as the best way of achieving this arrangement.

As a delegate to the Constitutional Convention, Hamilton had argued that the president should serve for life and that the states should subordinate themselves to the federal government. Given the incredible power that Great Britain enjoyed at the time, it made sense to Hamilton that America should model itself as closely as possible upon the English plan. Jefferson once wrote that Hamilton was "so bewitched and perverted by the British example as to be under thorough conviction that corruption was essential to the government of a nation."

Hamilton enjoyed significant support in the Congress, where many of the representatives and senators liked to think of themselves as a new generation of noble aristocrats. They called themselves Federalists because they believed in a strong federal government. Even Washington—who was known to ride around New York in a grand carriage draped with servants and drawn by no less than six horses—was partial to Hamilton's philosophy. Thomas Jefferson, needless to say, was not.

To Jefferson, Alexander Hamilton was a dangerous man who symbolized the corruption of government. Hamilton's America was about commerce and profit and not about the liberty and the empowerment of the people that were at the heart of the Declaration of Independence. To Hamilton, Jefferson was an out-of-touch idealist. The two men were destined to lock horns. Their conflict led directly to the emergence of party politics in America—with Hamilton's conservative Federalists on one side and Jefferson's more liberal Democratic-Republicans on the other.

"THE FATE OF HUMANITY"

Jefferson had joined the president's cabinet out of a sense of loyalty to George Washington and to the new government. But he soon felt himself surrounded by self-interested Federalists who were bent on using the power of their posts for personal gain. He watched aghast as Washington, Adams, and Hamilton added layers of pomp and affectation to the government. Jefferson was disgusted. He wrote,

> I took occasion at various times of expressing to General Washington my disappointment at these symptoms of a change of principle, and I thought them encouraged by the forms and ceremonies which I found prevailing . . . the levees, birthdays, the pompous cavalcade to the State House on the meeting of Congress, the formal speech from the throne, the procession of Congress in a body to re-echo the speech in an answer, etc.etc. . . . not at all in character with the simplicity of republican government, and looking as if wistfully to those of European courts.

In retrospect Jefferson's five years in France proved to be a blessing for democracy in America. He had seen for himself the direct effects of the monarchies in Europe. He had met kings and dined with blue-blooded aristocrats as well as witnessed the homeless, hungry masses in the streets. He had seen what becomes of a country when only a wealthy few are afforded liberty and justice. And he had watched France explode with revolution, unable to withstand the inequities any longer.

Now at home, he was shocked to find his fellow countrymen setting up a system that wasn't that much different from the one they had fought so bravely to free themselves of—with the exception that now *they* would be the aristocrats in charge. He was deeply disappointed. Historian Clay Jenkinson has said that

> France deepened his radicalism. He came back from France realizing that this isn't about ideas; this is about the fate of humanity, and that he had to give himself in an absolute commitment to the creation of something like a democratic social structure in the United States. And that prepared him psychically for the long struggle against Hamilton, Federalism and what amounts to a counterrevolution that occurred when he returned to this country.

Alexander Hamilton personified everything Jefferson disliked about what was happening to the country. Wendell Garrett notes, "Under Hamilton's aggressive leadership, financiers and speculators—'stockjobbers' as Jefferson called them—were getting a grip upon the federal government." Corruption, graft, and nepotism were eroding the heart of democracy before it even had a chance to prove itself. "Hamilton," Jefferson wrote, "was not only a monarchist but for a monarchy bottomed on corruption."

Having to work with Hamilton on an almost daily basis and watch his agenda take shape was almost too much for Jefferson to handle. His debilitating migraines started again. He grew depressed and longed to flee to the solitude of Monticello. After those wonderful years in France, he now found himself right back in the swirling pit of American politics, and he hated it.

Hamilton and his Federalists were the most formidable adversaries that Jefferson ever faced as a political leader. How he dealt with them, countered their tactics, and mounted a counterrevolution against them is one of the most fascinating episodes in the history of his leadership.

CONFLICT HAPPENS

The first thing we can learn from Jefferson's encounter with the zealous secretary of the Treasury is that even great leaders sometimes find themselves working alongside others with competing points of view. Whether it's a clash of personalities, values, or vision—or all three, in the case of Jefferson and Hamilton—conflict does happen. No leader, however accomplished or talented in people skills, is immune from it.

Thomas Jefferson once told a story about a dinner he gave in 1791, shortly after assuming his post in the State Department. Vice President Adams was there, as was Alexander Hamilton. After "the cloth was removed" and "conversation began," Adams remarked how he admired the British constitution. "Purge that constitution of its corruption," Adams maintained, "and give to its popular branch equality of representation, and it would be the most perfect constitution ever devised by the wit of man."

At that point Hamilton corrected him, "Purge it of its corruption, and give to its popular branch equality of representation and it would become an impracticable government; as it stands at present, with all its supposed defects, it is the most perfect government which ever existed." That likely made Jefferson quite uncomfortable, but Hamilton didn't stop there. That same evening Hamilton asked Jefferson about some paintings he had hanging in his apartment.

> The room being hung around with a collection of the portraits of remarkable men, among them were those of Bacon, Newton, and Locke. Hamilton asked me who they were. I told him they were my trinity of the three greatest men the world had ever produced, naming them. He paused for some time: "The greatest man," said he, "that ever lived was Julius Caesar."

That response was enough to make Jefferson's skin crawl. Caesar was, after all, a military leader who had brought about the end of the Roman democratic Republic and was named dictator for life (right before being assassinated in 44 B.C.). You can just imagine what Jefferson must have thought about Hamilton after this conversation! As far as Jefferson was concerned, Alexander Hamilton was a dictator-in-waiting.

Though no successful leader delights in personal conflict, it is something with which he or she must come to terms. Jefferson was as courteous as he could be to Hamilton. He tried to avoid situations that might cause friction and kept a polite distance. And that seemed to be effective—for a while.

We can't always work exclusively with people whom we like or admire, who make us happy or inspire us. Frequently we find ourselves forced to deal with people who do just the opposite. Such is the reality of human relations in any organization. Leaders attempt to respond to this inevitable challenge with civility, maturity, and patience—keeping the big picture and end goals in mind.

GET YOUR MESSAGE OUT THERE

It didn't take long before the private disagreements between Hamilton and Jefferson evolved into a public feud in the newspapers. In his *Gazette of the United States,* which first appeared in 1789, editor John Fenno was unabashed in his support of the conservative Federalists. Hamilton and John Adams were regular contributors, and they used the paper as a way to promote their policies. Hamilton in particular, always writing behind the veil of a pseudonym, launched a series of relentless attacks against Jefferson in the paper.

But Jefferson, Madison, and their supporters had no medium through which to respond. So in 1791 they arranged for poet and journalist Philip Freneau (who had been a friend of Madison's in college) to edit a new, anti-Federalist paper in the capital city. Freneau's *National Gazette* was launched on October 31, 1791. Jefferson adamantly refused to write under a pseudonym and was unwilling to attack his opponents under his own name because he believed it diminished the respectability of his office and tarnished the president. He therefore implored his allies to take full advantage of the newspaper. "For God's sake," he told Madison, "take up your pen, select the most striking heresies, and cut Hamilton to pieces in the face of the public."

The two periodicals waged a bitter battle over issues and personalities—now referred to by historians as the "Newspaper War." The insults, editorials, and bald-faced propaganda that filled their pages marks the beginning of partisan politics in America. And Jefferson was right there in the thick of it, orchestrating things behind the scenes to help fight that media war.

The lesson for aspiring leaders is clear: Get your message out there. Use whatever resources that are available to you to make your position known. Whether it is a school newspaper, a community newsletter, a local weekly, an Internet webpage, or any number of other media outlets that exist today, seize opportunities to advance your position.

DON'T UNDERESTIMATE THE POWER OF SHARED VALUES

The Newspaper War raged on throughout 1792. President Washington was distressed to see the feud cause a deep rift in his cabinet, and he urged Hamilton and Jefferson to lay their differences aside and work together. But the two men could not be reconciled. Their visions were just too incompatible.

As Washington's term drew to a close, he vowed not to stand for reelection. Like Jefferson, he had had enough of the nasty side of politics and wanted nothing more than to return to the peace of Mount Vernon. But without the ever-popular General at the helm many believed the Union would not hold, and the United States would split into competing factions. There was a genuine fear that the Newspaper War would become a very real conflict in the streets. Hamilton and Jefferson finally convinced Washington to stay on, and he was reelected for another four years.

The arguments that pulled Washington's team apart, however, did not let up in his second term. If anything, they grew worse. Hamilton was firm in his belief that Jefferson's obsession with the "voice of the people" stood in the way of realizing a strong America. And Jefferson was convinced that Hamilton's schemes "flowed from principles adverse to liberty." Ultimately, their differences reflected their opposing values.

Historian Joseph Ellis has written that "Hamilton was the kind of man who might have been put on earth by God to refute all the Jeffersonian values. Dashing and direct in his demeanor, Hamilton possessed all the confidence of a military leader accustomed to command, just the kind of explicit exercise of authority Jefferson found so irritating."

This aspect of their conflict illustrates a key point. In any organization, factions are likely to form along lines of belief, with people of similar values gravitating toward each other. Don't underestimate the power of shared beliefs to bring people together and, equally, the absence of similar values to pull people apart. It may not always be possible to avoid such situations, but being aware of them early on may allow you to minimize conflict.

As a leader you should make it a point to be aware of how values are affecting the web of relationships in your organization.

CHARACTER VERSUS LOYALTY

In his bid to challenge Hamilton and the Federalists, Jefferson found himself in an awkward situation. He and Hamilton were, after all, members of the same administration—they were on the same team. And yet they had very different goals in mind. Hamilton worked earnestly to re-create a British-style aristocracy in America, with a proactive federal government that benefited the "rich and the well-born." Jefferson, on the other hand, wanted to see the United States bring to life a true social democracy in which such vestiges of old-world privilege were done away with once and for all.

Historian Merrill Peterson has written that Jefferson was denounced as "the real enemy of the administration he pretended to serve. His role was not an easy one—a Janus in the cabinet according to the Hamiltonians—and but for his loyalty to President Washington he would have resigned his office."

It was that loyalty that kept Jefferson going for so long. But he finally reached the point where he couldn't rationalize staying at his post any longer. It was as if he were playing a game he could never win because he was playing on the wrong team. The frustration deepened his contempt for public office. "Politics," he wrote, "has become everything I hate."

In the summer of 1793 Jefferson tendered his resignation to the President. Out of respect for Washington he agreed to stay on until December, after which time he planned to leave politics for good and head home to Monticello. "The motion of my blood no longer keeps time with the tumult of the world," he said to Madison. "It leads me to seek for happiness in the lap and love of my family, in the society of my neighbors and my books, in the wholesome occupations of my farm and my affairs."

Loyalty is a defining characteristic of a powerful leader, but it should not be given blindly. Most important, it should never be allowed to eclipse a commitment to one's own values and principles.

Thomas Jefferson revered George Washington, there is no doubt. But for him to continue as a member of Washington's cabinet and work alongside Alexander Hamilton was no longer tenable. It wasn't his sense of loyalty that was at stake but his own character and peace of mind. It is a sign of a *lack of leadership* to stay in a position that contradicts your values, your vision, and everything you stand for.

True leaders refuse to sacrifice their character and self-respect in the name of loyalty to anyone.

MAKING CHANGES FROM WITHIN AND WITHOUT

Approaches to generating change in an organization or team can come from two directions—from within or without. As a member of Washington's cabinet, Jefferson spent years trying to effect change from within.

While serving the President with one hand, with the other he had conspired with Madison and the Democratic-Republicans in Congress. He had helped to establish an anti-Federalist newspaper that spoke out against the very administration in which he served. He had advocated policies as secretary of the state that he felt best expressed the values of his own position. And he had appealed directly to the President in an attempt to curb Hamilton's exercise of power. He had done what he could do. But in the end, this approach never produced the results Jefferson hoped it would. As the secretary of state, he was simply no match for Hamilton and the Federalist-dominated Congress.

So Jefferson resigned his office and left the scene. He didn't allow loyalty to trump his self-respect. He went into retirement in January 1794 and ultimately used the seclusion and peace of Monticello as a base from which to launch a counterrevolution against the Federalists. He took the second approach—to bring about change from without—which proved to be considerably more effective.

Unable to accomplish his objectives from within Washington's administration, Jefferson retreated, regrouped, and devised an innovative plan of action. His goals—to neutralize Hamilton's Federalists and promote a real democratic government in America—remained the same; only his approach changed. Historian Joyce Appleby has written that Jefferson championed "a radical political movement, mobilized to save the American Revolution. . . . When Jefferson threw off the constraints of his office and took his principles out of doors to an electorate unused to partisan politics, he did what had never been done before."

Leaders know that every conflict presents a different opportunity. Unwilling to compromise their character or their goals, they purposefully keep their plans fluid and able to respond to changing conditions. It is a timeless precept that every great leader knows well: The means must be kept flexible to achieve the ends.

COMMITTED TO LEADERSHIP

Jefferson was forthright in his desire to leave public life. Aside from a few brief visits, he had been away from Monticello for ten long years. He was ready to go home. He was fifty years old when he retired and went home to the mountains of Virginia—the same age his father had been when he passed away. That fact must have crossed his mind as he began to think of himself as destined for quiet, peaceful seclusion on his mountaintop, participating in the political fray only from a distance.

But make no mistake, Jefferson was not about to abandon his country to Hamilton and the Federalists. The more they went unchallenged, the more tyranny would be allowed to get a foothold in America. "I will not suffer my retirement," he wrote to President Washington, "to be clouded by the slanders of a man whose history, from the moment at which history can stoop to notice him, is a tissue of machinations against the liberty of the country." Even in his retirement, Jefferson resolved to influence the direction of the United States.

A RETIRED FARMER

Jefferson arrived home in early January 1794. Over the next few months, as winter thawed and gave way to a glorious Virginia spring, he zealously threw himself into architecture, writing, and farming. Ever the sentimentalist, he played up the romance of his newfound freedom in letters to friends. He said in one, "I return to farming with an ardor which I scarcely knew in my youth, and which has got the better entirely of my love of study. Instead of writing ten or twelve letters a day, which I have been in the habit of doing as a thing of course, I put off answering my letters now, farmer-like, till a rainy day."

At times he boasted of his isolation: "In the retired canton where I am, I learn little of what is passing; pamphlets I see never; papers but a few, and the fewer the happier." And he made clear his resolve to remain in the "domestic bliss" of Monticello. "Politics, a subject I never loved, and now hate," he wrote John Adams. "I have no ambition to govern men; no passion which would lead me to delight to ride in a storm."

But for all his talk of retirement and seclusion, Jefferson never hesitated to weigh in on the issues of the day; though he often refrained from reading the newspapers, he was kept informed about the latest domestic and international news by Madison and other friends. Jefferson had been retired for less than six weeks, for example, when he wrote to Adams offering his prescription for how the government should proceed:

> This I hope will be the age of experiments in government, and that their basis will be founded on principles of honesty, not of mere force. We have seen no instance of this since the days of the Roman republic, nor do we read of any before that. Either force or corruption has been the principle of every modern government. . . . If ever the morals of a people could be made the basis of their own government, it is our case.

In another letter that spring, the self-described retired farmer described his deep concerns about the present course of the nation's leadership.

> In place of that noble love of liberty and republican government which carried us triumphantly thro' the war, an Anglican monarchical, & aristocratical party has sprung up, whose avowed object is to draw over us the substance, as they have already done the forms, of the British government. . . . Against us are the Executive, the Judiciary, two out of three branches of the legislature, all the officers of the government, all who want to be officers, all timid men who prefer the calm of despotism to the boisterous sea of liberty, British merchants & Americans trading on British capitals, speculators and holders in the banks and public funds, a contrivance invented for the purposes of corruption, and for assimilating us in all

> things to the rotten as well as the sound parts of the British model. . . . In short, we are likely to preserve the liberty we have obtained only by unremitting labors & perils. But we shall preserve them.

Though he spent more of this time thinking about crops than politics, Jefferson never abandoned his commitment to setting things right. He kept a watchful eye on events in the nation's capital, and made it known to those close to him that, though retired, he would not abdicate his leadership in the fight to establish a true democratic republic in America.

"MORE CRAFTY"

Jefferson's retirement from public life needs to be understood in the context of American politics at the time. Historian Joseph Ellis explains, "Incantations of virtuous retirement to rural solitude after a career of public service were familiar and even formulaic refrains within the leadership class of eighteenth-century America, none more so than within the Virginia dynasty." Jefferson's Federalist critics charged that he was going home merely to "lick his wounds, storing up his energies for the inevitable assault on the presidency, posturing as the retired farmer."

Time would show that their intuition had some merit. Everyone involved, even Jefferson himself, understood that he was a more viable leader—and thus more of a threat to the conservative Federalists—as a farmer than he was as an actor on an unfriendly political stage. So beginning in 1794 he painted himself into the bucolic scene of Monticello. He became a student of agriculture. He talked of potatoes and flowers. He was fascinated by the technology of a plow.

"In the eighteenth-century," historian Clay Jenkinson has said, "it was required of all political figures to pretend that they didn't want the office. General Washington did it, Adams did it.

But they of course all wanted office very badly. And Jefferson was no different than the others. In fact, in some regards, Jefferson was more ambitious than the others—but more crafty."

In modern-day terms, Jefferson fashioned himself as an outsider, a man of the people, and distanced himself from the power-hungry career politicians in the nation's capital.

Jefferson never imagined himself as a leader of the bankers and big-business types who grabbed the reins of power to enrich themselves. He saw himself instead as a champion of the people, whom he envisioned as a sprawling nation of self-reliant, democratic citizen farmers. What better way to demonstrate his solidarity with them and to position himself in direct opposition to Hamilton's wealthy Federalists than to resign public office and retire to a life of farming?

On another level Jefferson demonstrated an intuitive understanding of the nature of executive leadership. He showed that his credibility and authority would be strengthened if he let others appeal to him for direction and call him out of retirement, rather than trying to force his leadership on the scene.

To be sure, Thomas Jefferson was sincere about staying out of the fray. He truly enjoyed overseeing his crops and designing additions to Monticello. But even more than that, he was absolutely determined to combat the Federalist agenda and champion democracy. He was willing to do whatever it took to help lead that assault, even if it meant reentering the "storm" of political life—which, in the end, it did.

THE JAY TREATY

As Jefferson busied himself with his crops and the production of nails in his new nailery at Monticello, President Washington sent John Jay to London to negotiate a new treaty with England. Because the Americans had little means to enforce existing peace terms, the British were in clear violation of the eleven-year-old Treaty of Paris (which had brought the Revolutionary War to an end). The British continued to operate military outposts in the American West and to seize U.S. ships at sea. Washington hoped that a renewed diplomatic effort might lessen the hostilities that still remained.

The result of John Jay's efforts—a treaty signed between England and the United States in November 1794—was nothing short of a disaster as far as Jefferson was concerned. The disappointing terms of the treaty allowed England to continue to detain American ships and to force captured U.S. sailors to serve in the British army. In nearly every aspect the treaty was a solid win for the British. Jefferson described the Jay Treaty as "an execrable thing" for it compromised the nation's liberties in the name of commerce; the United States made enormous sacrifices to maintain profitable relations. He saw it as a reversal of everything the Declaration of Independence had stood for. Many Americans agreed. Jay was burned in effigy throughout the country, and Hamilton—not surprisingly, the treaty's most vocal supporter—was peppered with rocks by an angry mob.

When the treaty came up before Congress for ratification the following year, Jefferson worked diligently from Monticello to drum up opposition, but to no avail. Given the public outcry, the President was reluctant to sign the treaty into law. But thanks to Hamilton's insistence Washington gave his stamp of approval in the summer of 1795. The Federalists and the British had won a definitive victory.

Thomas Jefferson's defeat in the political struggle that surrounded the 1795 Jay Treaty offers students of leadership a series of salient lessons to consider.

1. **Accepting your defeat does not mean wallowing in disappointment. It means recognizing that your victory has merely been delayed. You will fight again.**
2. **Study the reasons for your opponent's success; look for signs of strength and weakness. Is there an opening you can take advantage of?**
3. **Step back and look at the game itself. How was it played? Have the rules changed?**
4. **Reevaluate your tactics. What could you have done differently?**
5. **With this knowledge, begin to prepare your team immediately for the next encounter. "And in the meantime, patience."**

LESSONS IN THE FACE OF DEFEAT

From his vantage point at Monticello Thomas Jefferson learned a great deal by studying how Hamilton and his band of bankers and merchants had worked the system to their advantage. He concluded that it was the President's popularity alone which had secured them approval for the controversial Jay Treaty. But after Washington was out of the picture, then where would they be? In their triumph the Federalists had revealed their greatest weakness. After explaining this in a letter to Monroe, Jefferson counseled, "In the meantime, patience." Joseph Ellis writes that what Jefferson saw clearly in the wake of the Jay Treaty debate was that the resolution of the questions raised by the treaty had been reached by a new kind of politics in which both sides acknowledged that success depended upon an appeal to popular opinion. Washington's nearly unassailable popularity had given the Federalists a decided edge in this particular contest. But once the game had been defined in these terms—that is, once republicanism became more democratic in character—the Federalists were doomed.

"A COLLECTOR OF PROTÉGÉS"

During his brief retirement at Monticello Jefferson relied a great deal on his younger friends, James Madison and James Monroe especially. But these men were more than just friends. Besides being his eyes and ears, and constantly providing him with information, they were his trusted protégés. Thomas Jefferson was the consummate mentor—always ready to counsel, challenge, encourage, and empower younger men. It proved to be one of the keys to his excellent leadership.

"To understand Jefferson," historian Clay Jenkinson has said, "you need to know that he was a collector of protégés. He could never have achieved what he did without able-bodied men who yielded their own characters to his. They seemed to recognize that there was some type of greatness in Jefferson that simply deserved that support."

And support him they did. In fact, Madison was such an active promoter of Jefferson's pro-democracy agenda that Federalists in the Congress were known to refer to Madison as "the General" and Jefferson as "the Generalissimo."

Great leaders know that developing protégés is an essential aspect of their success and responsibility. They are willing to invest time to serve as role models, to advise, to protect, to educate, and to befriend others—the ultimate goal being the training of new leaders who will carry their program forward into the future.

Consider the fact that Thomas Jefferson eventually served two terms as president of the United States. His tenure was immediately followed by two terms of James Madison in the office, followed by two terms of James Monroe. Twenty-four of the first thirty-five years of the American presidency therefore were guided by the Jeffersonian vision—and particularly, by three men from central Virginia. Cultivating protégés is a proven and reliable way to broaden the scope of your leadership and to extend the influence of your agenda.

"THE SECOND OFFICE"

Jefferson's astute protégé James Madison led the effort to designate the retired Monticello farmer a presidential candidate in 1796. George Washington was committed to stepping down after his second term, and John Adams was already gearing up to take his place, with strong backing from Hamilton's Federalist machine. The Democratic-Republicans had but one logical choice: Jefferson.

In keeping with the political customs of the time, Jefferson refrained from campaigning personally. He left it up to his protégés to muster support and get out the vote. The final tally was counted in early 1797. Jefferson lost to Adams by just three electoral votes. As the runner-up—according to the rules of the day—that meant that he would serve as Adams' vice president, a position he was actually pleased to accept. "A more tranquil and unoffending station could not have been found for me," he wrote. "It will give me philosophical evenings in the winter, and rural days in summer. . . . The second office of the government is honorable and easy, the first is but a splendid misery."

Although publicly Jefferson was pleased with the subordinate position it being a way to maintain the leadership of his party without enduring the conflict so often found in the spotlight, privately he was most likely very disappointed. The result of the election promised at least four more years of Federalist schemes to endure.

In March 1797 he traveled to Philadelphia to watch the inauguration of John Adams. Jefferson's efforts to take on the pro-British, antidemocratic forces in the government appeared to have been dealt yet another blow, and he found himself once again serving in an administration that he opposed. In retrospect, however, Jefferson's razor-close, second-place finish in the election was just the precursor to a triumphant victory. Two significant facts emerged from that historic contest that would set the stage for a successful counterrevolution.

First, the Democratic-Republicans had run a terrific campaign and mobilized an impressive, nationwide opposition to the Federalists. They had come to represent an irrefutable threat to Hamilton and his wealthy constituency. History would show that this was the last great electoral victory for the Federalists. Second, Jefferson had solidified his position as the undeniable leader of the opposition party. He had thrown off the image of a retired farmer and set aside his distaste for political life to heed the call of duty one more time. For the first time in his life he stood as the potential leader of his country—a possibility that would soon be realized.

"THE LOSS OF LIBERTY"

Of the major events that transpired during Jefferson's four-year term as vice president to Adams, one episode in particular best features his executive leadership abilities—the tumult surrounding the Alien and Sedition Acts of 1798.

In retaliation for the pro-British Jay Treaty, which in effect gave the English navy carte blanche, the French wreaked havoc at sea by ambushing American vessels and confiscating cargo. Adams' attempts to initiate a treaty with the French had been soundly rejected, and the United States rumbled with the talk of a possible war. Federalist politicians and newspaper editors fanned the flames of war hysteria, for they saw in the crisis, as historian Wendell Garrett points out, an opportunity to stamp out political opposition at home:

> An epidemic of galloping xenophobia led to repressive legislation with the aim of deporting French propagandists, English infidels, and Irish agitators. In the summer of 1798 the Federalist Congress against the advice of cooler heads in the party pushed their advantage hard and passed the Alien and Sedition Acts, designed to choke off agitation and to stifle criticism of the administration and its policies.

With passage of the Alien and Sedition Acts, the reactionary conservatives in Congress essentially nullified the Bill of Rights and launched an assault on civil liberties—all in the name of a supposed war. In an insightful comment that has stood the test of time James Madison wrote to Jefferson, "Perhaps it is a universal truth that the loss of liberty of home is to be charged to provisions against danger real or pretended from abroad." The threat of war, therefore, gives powerful leaders an excuse to limit or put an end to individual freedoms.

People across the country were fined, arrested, and jailed for speaking out against the Federalist government. Anti-Federalist newspapers were closed down. "Radical," pro-Jefferson editors were jailed or went into hiding. Immigrants were rounded up and deported for spurious reasons. Protestors against the acts were dealt with harshly by police. Thomas Jefferson was outraged. He viewed these actions as nothing short of a "Federalist reign of terror."

After all, Jefferson was the man who had written twenty years before, "The opinions of men are not the object of civil government, nor under its jurisdiction." But he had lived to see the democratic government he helped to create become a weapon of tyranny. Shortly after Congress passed the heinous laws he wrote with anxiety, "There is no event, however atrocious, which may not be expected." The Alien and Sedition Acts were proof that Hamilton, Adams, and the other Federalists were intent on using the machinery of the federal government to roll back the freedoms that had been gained during the revolution.

STRATEGIC RETREAT

As the leader of the opposition, people turned to Jefferson for a swift counteraction to the abominable Alien and Sedition Acts. But he had nothing to say. As a matter of fact, the Vice President quietly packed his bags in Philadelphia and went home to Monticello. And there he stayed quiet for two months.

Americans across the country looked to Jefferson for inspiration and leadership—anything that might signal a defense against the Federalist onslaught. But Jefferson remained taciturn. His silence in the face of such urgency was intensely frustrating for many. But as we now know, he was thinking, planning, and devising a strategy.

Jefferson grappled with the dilemma of how best to respond to these offensive laws. How should he lead the fight against them? After some sober meditation on the subject in the peaceful setting at Monticello, he picked up the weapon he wielded best, his pen. In so doing, he responded to a crisis with one of his greatest talents—a move he had *not* made some years before as governor during the American Revolution. But now, with decades of leadership experience behind him, he brought his most formidable strength to bear. We each have our own innate or learned talents, and should not hesitate to rely on them when the need arises.

Over the next few weeks, through the late summer and early autumn of 1798, Jefferson wrote an historic manifesto that took a hard line against the Alien and Sedition Acts. He declared the laws unconstitutional and concluded that the individual states had a right therefore not to enforce them.

For Jefferson it was this simple: Because these federal laws violated the rights protected by the Constitution, the state governments had an obligation to deem the Alien and Sedition Acts "void and of no force." He surreptitiously passed the manifesto (which went *unsigned*) to friends, who in turn submitted the document in the Kentucky legislature. Secrecy was a high priority, for Jefferson could have been arrested and even impeached for criticizing the government. After some minor amendments and debate, the Kentucky state assembly adopted the historic declarations in November—since known as the Kentucky Resolutions. A similar though less radical version of the resolutions were written by Madison and adopted by the Virginia legislature a few weeks later.

Like every tyrannical regime, the Federalist government relied on fear and apathy to extend their influence and power. As long as the American people were kept in alarm over the threat of a supposed war and were made to believe that these transgressions on their freedoms were somehow necessary, the Federalists could continue to eat away at the sanctity of the Bill of Rights. Jefferson feared that unless checked the Alien and

Sedition Acts would be only the first steps toward the creation of a corrupt American monarchy.

The Federalists also depended on the fact that most people were convinced that they could do little to stem the oppressive tide even if they wanted to—that Hamilton and his supporters were simply too wealthy and too powerful to fight. Jefferson refused to accept this. He demonstrated that the American people were not afraid to take on the reactionary Federalist machine; and that they were not intimidated or complacent when it came to protecting their liberties.

THE STATES RIGHTS LEGACY

The Kentucky and Virginia Resolutions laid the foundation for what would eventually become known as the "doctrine of states rights." As such, the resolutions have been used and abused by generations of Americans. It's important to point out that Jefferson's chief concern in responding to the Alien and Sedition Acts as the leader of the opposition party—to quote Dumas Malone—"was not to aggrandize state power for its own sake, but to safeguard the freedom of individuals." Malone continues,

> To base a states-rights position on [the Kentucky and Virginia Resolutions of 1798] without reference to human rights would be to disregard their central purpose. They must be viewed in no vacuum but in their own setting of time and circumstances. While [Jefferson] was undoubtedly concerned to preserve his party and to check what he regarded as a trend toward consolidation, he was not seeking primarily to safeguard local interests, and certainly not vested interests, but the freedom of all men everywhere to think as they liked and speak as they thought. Emphasis should be laid not on the weapon he used, but on the ends he sought.

Thomas Jefferson was not, as some like to believe, an absolute extremist on the issue of states' rights. He believed, for example, that the federal government should assume authority for the commerce of all states. And he obviously thought that a federal government and its national laws were important factors in preserving the freedoms of Americans.

The issue was fundamentally a practical matter for Jefferson. His goal was always the same: maximizing a citizen's rights to life, liberty, and the pursuit of happiness. That is why he thought the U.S. Constitution was incomplete without the Bill of Rights. Both the federal and state governments had roles to play in protecting and ensuring those rights. And he clearly believed that it behooved them to check each other's transgressions.

KEEP YOUR PLANS FLUID, GOALS FIRM

Jefferson explained his strategy of opposition to the Alien and Sedition Acts in a letter:

> For the present I should be for resolving the alien and sedition laws to be against the constitution and merely void, and for addressing the other states to obtain similar declarations; and I would not do anything at this moment which should commit us further, but reserve ourselves to shape our future measure, or no measure, by the events which may happen.

Here again we see that as a great leader, Jefferson chose the means which would most effectively secure the ends he valued. He kept his goal firm and his plan fluid, able to adapt as circumstances changed.

In the end it wasn't an actual form of government—state or federal—that was to be the prevailing concern for Jefferson but, rather, the promotion and protection of the principles of freedom.

"OUR FUTURE MEASURE"

Another important lesson we can draw from Jefferson's counterattack of 1798 is this: When presented with a critical situation an effective leader does not *react,* he or she *responds.* A reaction is too often based on emotion and snap judgments. A response is a well-thought-out, reasoned address to the situation that signals an organized plan.

The Kentucky Resolutions represented just such an approach to the Alien and Sedition Acts. Jefferson's manifesto was an indicator that the states were not going to sit by and let the Federalists in Philadelphia eradicate the freedoms that had been guaranteed in the Constitution. Jefferson refused to allow himself to be compromised by the urgent calls for action that were coming from around the country. He again kept his cool and methodically crafted a brilliant countermove. He displayed incredible patience and forethought. In true Jeffersonian fashion, he thought logically about the situation from a variety of angles, put his best talents to work for the cause, and initiated a counteroffensive using trusted allies.

Jefferson was encouraged by the positive reaction among the American people to the Kentucky and Virginia Resolutions. He believed that the public was awakening to facts that he had known for years—that the Federalists were out to line their own pockets, not to empower the people, and that they were pri-

In less than two years Jefferson had gone from being a farmer to the national leader of a fight against tyrannical forces in the American government. "In the darkest days of Federalist reaction," Wendell Garrett writes, "Jefferson's function was to inspire, to motivate, to stimulate, to clarify. He wanted his friends and followers to understand the fundamental issues and to act upon them in the light of reason. He placed all his faith in the education of the public."

marily concerned with advancing the liberties of only a wealthy few. In March 1799 Jefferson wrote these now famous words,

> The spirit of 1776 is not dead. It has only been slumbering. The body of the American people is substantially republican. But their virtuous feelings have been played on by some fact with more fiction; they have been the dupes of artful maneuvers and made for a moment to be willing instruments in forging chains for themselves. But time & truth have dissipated the delusion, & opened their eyes.

Jefferson the Statesman: Some Final Thoughts

In the ten years following his return from France in 1789 Jefferson saw his worst fears realized. Monarchy-leaning Federalists grabbed the national government and embarked on a campaign to gut the Constitution of the personal liberties it guaranteed U.S. citizens. He watched as Hamilton's pals grew richer and more powerful, while people were arrested in the streets for speaking their minds.

In mounting what became a counterrevolution against this despotism, Jefferson's vision and inspiration were invaluable. His leadership matured and his political skills rose to a new level of expertise. Though familiar with defeat, Jefferson refused to surrender. His tenacity, his faith in the promise of American democracy, and his allegiance to the spirit of 1776 would eventually overwhelm his adversaries, propel him into the White House, and change the course of world history.

- Great leaders have an instinctive sense of duty. It shapes their beliefs, their actions, and their character. An appreciation for responsibility is at the very core of who they are.
- No leader is immune to personal conflict. Even great leaders sometimes find themselves working alongside others with whom they disagree or don't get along. Respond to this inevitable challenge with civility, maturity, and patience.
- Never pass up an opportunity to get your message out there. Take advantage of the media.
- Be aware of how values are affecting the web of relationships in your organization.
- Never compromise your character, integrity, or self-respect in the name of personal loyalty.
- There are two ways to effect change: from within an organization or from without. Whatever approach you decide to take, remember that every scene of conflict presents a new opportunity to advance your agenda. Keep your plans fluid and your goals firm.
- Leaders strengthen their credibility and power when they allow themselves to be called into service, rather than forcing their authority on others.
- Accepting defeat does not mean wallowing in disappointment. It means recognizing that your victory has merely been delayed. "In the meantime, patience."

- Study the reasons for your opponent's success; look for signs of strength and weakness. Reexamine the nature of the contest, and reevaluate your tactics.
- Be a collector of protégés. Invest your time and energy in developing promising young leaders.
- An effective leader does not react; he or she *responds.* A reaction is too often based on emotion and snap judgments. A response is a well-thought-out, reasoned address to the situation that signals an organized plan.

CHAPTER 9

JEFFERSON THE PRESIDENT

A just and solid republican government maintained here will be a standing monument and example for the aim and imitation of the people of other countries.

By the time the presidential election of 1800 rolled around, Jefferson had positioned himself as the indisputable leader of the anti-Federalist, democratic forces in America. He was the obvious candidate to again take on John Adams, who was vying for a second term. After one of the most divisive and bitter elections in U.S. history, Jefferson was elected president by a slim margin. The victory was sweet, and he described his win over the Federalists as a revolution no less important than that of 1776. Subsequently, he served two terms as the nation's chief executive from 1801 to 1809. Like nearly every other president who has served more than one term, the first was decidedly more successful than the second.

As president, Thomas Jefferson led the way in overturning the aristocratic tenor of the federal government. He championed instead a limited, more frugal government that worked to protect the civil liberties of its citizens. With the help of his party members who had won a majority in both houses of Congress, Jefferson abolished taxes, initiated a plan to pay down the national debt, and downsized the federal bureaucracy.

His tenure was not without adversity, however. While in the White House Jefferson faced a now historic attack from the partisan press. The country was captivated by published accounts of a rumored sexual affair with one of his slaves, Sally Hemings. That controversy continues to be the source of heated debate two hundred years later. Jefferson's years as president are also noteworthy for the Louisiana Purchase, which doubled the size of the United States. During this period Jefferson reached the pinnacle of his political career and manifested some of his most brilliant attributes as a leader.

THE ELECTION OF 1800

Jefferson's Kentucky Resolutions of 1798 were not enough to check the gross affronts to liberty perpetrated under the Alien and Sedition Acts. But the manifesto was a resounding rallying cry against the Federalists. When the campaign for president began in 1800, the country's Democratic-Republicans looked to Jefferson for leadership. He did not disappoint them and gave the go-ahead for his candidacy.

Federalists and their advocates assailed Jefferson in the media. The conservatives, who were wary of too much freedom in America, believed that Jefferson's democratic liberalism would surely bring chaos and cause the downfall of the government. Hamilton wrote that Jefferson was "too much in earnest in his democracy" and that his policies would lead to "universal bankruptcy and beggary [and] starving in the streets."

Even more alarming was the mudslinging of some religious leaders who all but called Jefferson the Antichrist. As one member of the clergy wrote just prior to the election, supporting "the principles of Mr. Jefferson would destroy religion, introduce immorality, and loosen all the bonds of society. . . . To vote for Jefferson is no less than a rebellion against God."

The charges were sensationalistic and malicious. Yet Jefferson refused to respond to them. As he saw it, they were lies not worthy of a rebuttal. "I know that I might have filled the courts of the United States with actions for these slanders," he wrote, "and have ruined perhaps many persons who are not innocent. But this would be no equivalent to the loss of character. I leave them, therefore, to the reproof of their own consciences. If these do not condemn them, there will yet come a day when the false witness will meet a judge who has not slept over his slanders."

In an effort to nail down the critical support of New York State, Jefferson chose as his running mate Aaron Burr, a powerful New York senator. But when the votes were counted in late 1800, Jefferson and Burr had each received 73 electoral votes. Though Adams and his Federalists had been soundly defeated, the race for president had ended in a tie. Confusion and an embittered debate followed, made all the worse by Burr's refusal to defer to Jefferson even though Burr had not been the candidate for president.

Following the provisions of the Constitution, a runoff election was held in the House of Representatives. After nearly forty tied ballots, Jefferson at last won the election. The key to his victory, surprisingly, was his arch rival, Alexander Hamilton—who disliked Burr even more than he did Jefferson. Under Hamilton's leadership, the Federalists swung their votes away from Burr and handed Jefferson the presidency. Burr, who settled for the post of vice president, never forgot Hamilton's role in the election. In the summer of 1804, just three years later, Burr shot and fatally wounded Hamilton in a duel.

"THE BRIGHT CONSTELLATION"

Jefferson rightly interpreted his success in the election of 1800 as a revolutionary triumph of republican democracy over aristocratic despotism. The American experiment had gone astray under the leadership of the Federalist party, and the time had come to set the country back on track. Jefferson later wrote that

> the revolution of 1800 . . . was as real a revolution in the principles of our government as that of 1776 was in its form; not effected indeed by the sword, as that, but by the rational and peaceable instrument of reform, the suffrage of the people.

On the afternoon of March 4, 1801, Thomas Jefferson took the oath of office for president in the as-yet-unfinished Capitol Building in the nation's new capital city, Washington, D.C. Even before he delivered the inaugural address that day, he made it clear that his was to be a very different presidency from the two that had preceded it. Instead of riding in an elegant carriage pulled by six horses, Jefferson walked to the Capitol with only a few friends and supporters. He wore an unpretentious suit and shoes with laces instead of shiny buckles—symbolically distancing himself from the garish trimmings of patrician Federalists.

As expected, the soft-spoken orator was hard to hear during his historic address that day. Many of those present didn't even know what he had said until they read a copy of the speech in the newspapers. Aside from the less-than-stellar delivery it received, Jefferson's first inaugural address was in some ways as inspiring and visionary as the Declaration of Independence had been. That more Americans today aren't familiar with it is disappointing.

In this speech Jefferson reached out to the defeated Federalist party and called for harmony and cooperation in the government. "Every difference of opinion is not a difference of principle," he said. "We have called by different names brethren of the same principle. We are all republicans—we are all federalists."

In laying out the "essential principles of our government" that would guide his administration, he affirmed his faith in the principles of the Enlightenment. He called for "equal and exact justice for all men . . . peace, commerce and honest friendship with all nations—entangling alliances with none; the support of the state governments in all their rights . . . supremacy of the civil over the military authority . . . honest payment of our debts . . . freedom of religion; freedom of the press." He went on:

> These principles form the bright constellation which has gone before us, and guided our steps through an age of revolution and reformation. The wisdom of our sages and the blood of our heroes have been devoted to their attainment. They should be the creed of our political faith—the text of our civil instruction—the touchstone by which to try the services of those we trust; and should we wander from them in moments of error or alarm, let us hasten to retrace our steps and to regain the road which alone leads to peace, liberty, and safety.

Just over two weeks after his inauguration, Jefferson shared the delight of his party's victory in a memorable letter to his friend the minister and scientist Dr. Joseph Priestly.

> What an effort, my dear Sir, of bigotry in Politics & Religion have we gone through! The barbarians really flattered themselves they should be able to bring back the times of Vandalism, when ignorance put everything into the hands of power & priestcraft. . . . We can no longer say there is nothing new under the sun. For this whole chapter in the history of man is new. . . . The order & good sense displayed in this recovery from delusion, and in the momentous crisis which lately arose, really bespeak a strength of character in our nation which augurs well for the duration of our Republic; & I am

much better satisfied now of its stability than I was before it was tried.

The Jeffersonian counterrevolution had achieved success. After a decade of watching the Federalists contaminate the Constitution and the country with their antidemocratic policies, Jefferson and his party had finally won control of the government. The Federalists would never again win the White House, and by the 1820s their party had all but disintegrated. Jefferson, meanwhile, assumed the most powerful leadership position in the country. The gangly, bookish lawyer from the mountains of Virginia had become the executive leader of a promising young nation.

FOUR FROM THE INAUGURAL

Jefferson's leadership was never more impressive than during his first term as president of the United States—a period of florescence we can see evidence of even on the day of his inaugural, before he officially went to work. Here are four of the most striking qualities of leadership that Jefferson put to work on the day of his triumphant inauguration.

1. Create the Criteria

Before anyone else has an opportunity to do so, you should create the criteria by which your leadership is to be judged; otherwise, how will anyone (even you) know when you have succeeded in your post? Remember that you cannot measure effective leadership by the absence of difficulties or challenges, for they will always be present. Your priority when accepting a position of authority should be to immediately spell out the standards by which your leadership should be measured.

Thomas Jefferson did this in his inaugural address by listing the "essential principles of our government" and by adding that these should be "the touchstone by which to try the services of those we trust." By laying out the code that would shape his administration, he gave the people the criteria by which they could judge his accomplishments as president. As long as he remained faithful to those principles, he could claim the success of his tenure.

2. *Don't Be Afraid to Speak in General Terms*

There is a time and a place to present the specifics of your plan. There are other moments when your leadership is best served by speaking in general terms. Historian Joseph Ellis observes that "a crucial component of Jefferson's genius was his ability to project his vision of American politics at a level of generalization that defied specificity and in a language that seemed to occupy an altitude where one felt obliged to look up and admire without being absolutely certain about the details." Every successful politician in America since Jefferson has attempted to emulate that genius.

In defining your leadership for others, be willing to speak in general terms. This approach can be abused by those who practice it, but if used with integrity it can be a powerful way to express your vision and motivate others to join your cause.

3. *Make Symbolism Work for You*

Though he was dead set against the adoration of "nobility, wealth, and pomp" and detested lofty rituals, Jefferson graciously took part in the ceremony of the inauguration. But he did so on his own terms. He walked to the Capitol instead of being chauffeured in an extravagant carriage. He wore plain clothes as opposed to the ornate wardrobe of Federalist "royalty." He made it clear that he identified himself as a "man of the people" as opposed to the representative of a wealthy ruling class. Jefferson used symbolism to his advantage and communicated the democratic frugality that would characterize his leadership.

Effective leaders know how to make symbolism work for them. They understand that powerful messages can be communicated without saying a word. At the same time, great leaders respect the rituals and procedures that have meaning to others. Participation in time-honored customs that are in accord with your principles can also be a potent way to communicate your leadership.

4. Winning with Grace

As Jefferson demonstrated in his eloquent inaugural address, a victorious leader is always humble and ever conciliatory. He or she appeals to reason, moderation, and cooperation. I "humble myself before the magnitude of the undertaking," Jefferson said on that important day. "To you, then, gentlemen, who are charged with the sovereign functions of legislation, and to those associated with you, I look with encouragement for that guidance and support which may enable us to steer with safety the vessel in which we are all embarked amid the conflicting elements of a troubled world."

By so openly appealing to his listeners for their participation in government, Jefferson demonstrated his intention to create partnerships that could work for the greater good of the nation. Winning with grace means appealing with sincere humility for cooperation from the opposition.

"A STANDING MONUMENT"

Jefferson went to great lengths to separate the presidency from any resemblance to a monarchy. He refused any national celebrations of his birthday and would not allow his image to be used on currency. Among his first acts as president was to pardon everyone who had been imprisoned under the Sedition

Act for speaking out against the government. He strongly supported the free press, recognizing it as a critical element to the success of a democratic nation. He once wrote that

> no experiment can be more interesting than that we are now trying, which we trust will end in establishing the fact that man may be governed by reason and truth. Our first object should therefore be to leave open to him all the avenues to truth. The most effectual hitherto found is the freedom of the press. It is therefore the first shut up by those who fear the investigation of their actions.

Working with others of his party in the Congress, he also managed to abolish all domestic taxes while simultaneously paying down the national debt. These policies were in keeping with his philosophy of a thrifty administration. Jefferson believed that no government, federal or state, should overburden its citizens with taxes; equally important was his belief that the government should not be wasteful in its spending. To do so would be nothing less than a sign of corruption and would condemn otherwise free citizens to the chains of endless debt. In a powerful letter written in July 1816 Jefferson addressed this point in some detail.

> I am not among those who fear the people. They, and not the rich, are our dependence for continued freedom. And to preserve their independence, we must not let our rulers load us with perpetual debt. . . . If we run into such debts, as that we must be taxed in our meat and in our drink, in our necessaries and our comforts, in our labors and our amusements, for our callings and our creeds, as the people of England are, our people, like them, must come to labor sixteen hours in the twenty-four, give the earnings of fifteen of these to the

> government for their debts and daily expenses; and the sixteenth being insufficient to afford us bread, we must live, as they now do, on oatmeal and potatoes; have no time to think, no means of calling the mismanagers to account; but be glad to obtain subsistence by hiring ourselves to rivet their chains on the necks of our fellow-sufferers. . . . This is the tendency of all human governments. A departure from principle in one instance becomes a precedent for a second; that second for a third; and so on, till the bulk of the society is reduced to be mere automatons of misery, and to have no sensibilities left but for sinning and suffering. . . . And the fore horse of this frightful team is public debt. Taxation follows that, and in its train wretchedness and oppression.

Avoiding the devolution into corruption and despotism that had been the fate of every previous republic in history was a very real concern for Jefferson. The key to his solution was a limited government that remained small and responsive so that citizens would not be overburdened—all the while aiming to protect and strengthen their civil liberties. It was not just the future of America that was at stake but ultimately the principle of representative government itself.

"A just and solid republican government maintained here," he wrote with enthusiasm just two days after his inauguration, "will be a standing monument and example for the aim and imitation of the people of other countries; and I join with you in the hope and belief that they will see from our example that a free government is of all others the most energetic; that the inquiry which has been excited among the mass of mankind by our revolution and its consequences will ameliorate the condition of man over a great portion of the globe."

CHOOSING YOUR TEAM

To accomplish his goals and put American democracy back on course, Jefferson assembled a team that included some of the brightest and most qualified men of the time—men who also represented a new generation of leaders. Scholar Robert Johnstone has written that to be a member of Jefferson's party in 1801 "was in many places to be antiestablishment in outlook and background. Jefferson's appointees were new men, in many cases men who were challenging the established leadership in their communities. . . . While Adams' elite was dominated by financial, commercial, and trading interests, Jefferson's appointees more often reflected less-established economic interests."

It should be noted that Jefferson appointed no women to his cabinet. As he wrote to a friend, "the appointment of a woman to office is an innovation for which the public is not prepared, nor am I." No woman was appointed to a cabinet position in America until 1933.

President Jefferson named his closest ally and protégé, James Madison, secretary of state. And in one of the best moves he ever made in his political career, he selected the exceptional Albert Gallatin to head up the Treasury Department. Gallatin's meticulous accounting skills helped to curb spending and reduced the national debt by $14 million.

Jefferson chose two Northerners for key posts—Henry Dearborn as secretary of war and Levin Lincoln as attorney general. As Johnstone points out, these appointments were a calculated political maneuver on Jefferson's part to extend his base of support into the Federalist stronghold of New England.

Some of the most significant decisions leaders ever make involve deciding who will serve on their team of closest advisors. Jefferson displayed a remarkable skill for picking the right people. He selected intelligent, capable individuals who could work productively and harmoniously. He also chose people who would fortify his leadership, a crafty move by an experienced politician.

Jefferson was aware of his own strengths and weaknesses, and he found people who excelled in those areas where he did not. As Johnstone observes in the case of James Madison, "Madison's collaboration with Jefferson was close and marked by great mutual affection and respect. Madison's more cautious, practical and analytical mind provided an appropriate counterpoise to Jefferson's more impulsive and imaginative spirit. Together they made an excellent political team, each balancing the other's deficiencies while pursuing a common approach to policy."

MANAGING YOUR TEAM

As we might expect, Jefferson took a progressive approach to managing his administration. He evidenced a great deal of faith in his subordinates, both in his cabinet and in the Congress. Robert Johnstone writes that Jefferson

> never dictated policy positions to them; he only suggested. He never seemed to inflict his opinions upon them; he only insinuated them. Explicit demands were never employed where implicit methods could suffice. The President preferred to

use more informal methods of effecting his will through private conversations.

Besides shrinking the federal bureaucracy, Jefferson streamlined the workings of his own office. Unlike Adams and Washington, he did not convene weekly meetings of his cabinet. Time could be better spent and his team could be more productive, he concluded, by not compelling people to sit through regular meetings. Historian Joseph Ellis notes that

> on every working day each department head sent Jefferson a written summary of all decisions or issues in his area. Jefferson responded in writing, if possible on the same day, and also made himself available for individual conferences before his daily horseback ride at one o'clock. . . . This arrangement made the President, as Jefferson put it, "the hub of the wheel" with the business of the nation done at the rim, conveyed through the departmental spokes, but all supervised at the center.

Jefferson's managerial approach was fluid, informal, and ultimately based on empowering others and on keeping himself apprised of every important situation. His style was also intensely practical, as Johnstone suggests: "There was a strong current of pragmatism in Jefferson's conduct of government [that was] combined with a commitment to progressive change and an indifference to precedent and tradition."

BE YOUR OWN DIPLOMAT

In his first four years as president Thomas Jefferson displayed a masterful brilliance, applying the many lessons he had learned during more than thirty years in public service. His experiences as an attorney, legislator, governor, diplomat, and statesman combined to produce one of the highest-quality tenures in the history of the American presidency. At perhaps no other time in his life was Jefferson a more exceptional leader.

Johnstone comments that "Jefferson's presidency marked the pioneering effort in erecting a working model of presidential leadership characterized by persuasion and the cultivation of influence. . . . Jefferson may be said to have prefigured the modern presidency." One of Jefferson's most effective tools when it came to cultivating that influence was the White House dinner party, to which he often invited congressmen, foreign diplomats, and their wives.

One part of Jefferson's presidential philosophy was simple: Get people away from the trappings of their offices and duties, and bring them together in an informal, relaxed setting.

"I have always seen business done more easily and more amicably," Jefferson once wrote, "where the parties have met in a friendly way and at a private house where they would have the leisure and the dispositions to explain and approximate their opinions, than in a public place, confined to a particular hour, and pressed and interrupted by other business."

This approach to negotiations and relations he had learned as a student in Williamsburg and perfected as a diplomat in France. President Jefferson hosted three grand dinner parties each week and became something of a diplomat for his own administration. He even kept a record of the number of times each member of Congress had been invited to dinner, and with whom they had sat. Besides strengthening the alliances among the Jeffersonians and courting the support of Federalist opponents, the dinners also made it possible—as Joseph Ellis points out—for people to actually see the president, a rare opportunity in that era before photographs and television.

DRAW FORTH THE TALENTS OF OTHERS

Jefferson's conversational style at those dinner parties is worth considering, for it illustrates a skilled leader at work. Though a poor public orator, Jefferson was an expert conversationalist in intimate settings. He enjoyed telling stories. He loved to talk about books, horses, the weather, gardening, and of course, Virginia. Margaret Baynard Smith, who chronicled the social life in Washington during Jefferson's presidency, was a guest at many of those galas. In her flattering observations of Jefferson she noted that the President

> took the lead and gave the tone, with a tact so true and discriminating that he seldom missed his aim, which was to draw forth the talents and information of each and all of his guests, and to place every one in an advantageous light and by being pleased with themselves, be enabled to please others.

President Jefferson was supremely talented at directing a conversation in such a way that made others feels comfortable, got them talking about subjects that interested them, and showcased their talents and accomplishments. In conversation, as in other areas, the best leaders are consummate facilitators, adept at bringing out the very best in others.

When talking with others, make it a point to use their name, to ask them about themselves, to inquire about topics that appeal to them, and to put the spotlight on their achievements.

"HER NAME IS SALLY"

Though Jefferson's White House dinners were effective in generating support for his leadership, his presidency was certainly not immune from scandal.

On September 1, 1802, an article appeared in a Richmond, Virginia, newspaper, *The Recorder*, that had an immediate and long-lasting impact on public perception of Thomas Jefferson. The author of the piece was James Callender, who had at one time been a hired muckraker for the Jeffersonians. His scathing anti-Federalist attacks in the press had gotten him fined and briefly jailed under the Sedition Act. But by Jefferson's second year as president, Callender's loyalties had changed. Possibly angered over Jefferson's refusal to give him a job in his administration, Callender turned on the President with a vengeance. His article read in part:

> It is well known that the man, whom it delighteth the people to honor, keeps and for many years has kept, as his concubine, one of his slaves. Her name is Sally. By this wench Sally, our president has had several children. There is not an individual in the neighborhood of Charlottesville who does not believe the story and not a few who know it.

Callender charged that Jefferson had children by his slave Sally Hemings, who was his deceased wife's half-sister. Hemings was an enslaved seamstress at Monticello and also served as

Jefferson's chambermaid. His relationship with her had been a well-circulated rumor among some in the Charlottesville area for at least a few years. But this article quickly brought that gossip out into the open for the American public to consider—and consider it we have, for the last two hundred years.

As other newspapers picked up on the story, much of the country was rocked with titillating talk of "Tom and Sally." Conservative Federalists used the allegations to disgrace him personally. Jefferson's supporters defended him by denying any truth to the story. Thomas Jefferson himself, however, never denied the accusations either publicly or privately. He simply refused to talk about it. Some historians have scoured his thousands of letters for a denial, or anything that might sound like a denial, to the alleged affair; what there is remains ambiguous and by no means explicitly refers to Sally Hemings. He did complain at one point that newspapers were full of "false impressions," but as far as categorically disavowing the veracity of the story, he never said a word.

DNA AND DEBATE

In 1998 DNA tests established a genetic link between the Jefferson family and the descendants of Sally Hemings' son Eston. The study concluded that "the simplest and most probable" explanation is that Jefferson and Hemings had had children together. It's important to point out that the DNA tests did not, as many people mistakenly believe, absolutely prove that Jefferson was the father of Hemings' children. The study merely revealed a genetic link that (for most people, at least) lends a high probability to that conclusion.

The Thomas Jefferson Memorial Foundation, which operates Monticello and the International Center for Jefferson Studies, assembled a team of experts to review the historical evidence in light of the new DNA report. Among the evidence, they considered the facts that unlike nearly every other enslaved person at Monticello, Sally Hemings and all of her children were eventually freed from slavery; that Jefferson was present at Monticello when her children were conceived; that her children seemed to resemble Thomas Jefferson; that a close friend of Jefferson admitted to knowing of the relationship; and that a very strong oral history among the families of Sally Hemings' descendants corroborates the story. In January 2000 the foundation reported its findings—Thomas Jefferson was "most likely" the father of Sally Hemings' six children.

Many people, including most historians, appear to agree with that conclusion. They are willing to acknowledge that it's highly probable that Jefferson had a sexual affair with Hemings. But many other individuals, including some of Jefferson's white descendants, are not convinced. They insist the evidence is insufficient to make even probable conclusions. Some have gone further by denouncing the recent reports as politically correct "poppycock."

As vigorous studies continue on these issues, we can turn to questions about their significance from a leadership standpoint. We will see that, as has been the case with other major controversies surrounding Jefferson, we may learn valuable lessons from both his actions and his inactions.

RESPONDING TO PERSONAL ATTACKS

As the presidential campaign of 1800 had shown, Jefferson did not usually respond directly to scandalous allegations that were made in the press. It was his firm belief that doing so would serve to give the stories more attention and merit than they deserved. So he ignored them, leaving those who wrote and published the stories "to the reproof of their own consciences."

Historian Joseph Ellis notes that the Hemings stories in the opposition press did little to harm Jefferson's popularity. "The political damage to his presidency proved less serious than the lingering stigma that attached itself to his image with posterity. Jefferson's posture of total silence on the matter prevented any prolonged debate from feeding on itself." Despite all the hoopla in the press, the story died down, and Jefferson was overwhelmingly reelected to a second term just two years later. His silence seems to have served his political career well.

Sometimes leaders need to, and should, respond to personal attacks made by their opponents. Silence can often be seen by the public as an admission of guilt. Speaking up expresses a confidence of innocence and a willingness to see that the truth is told. Other times, leaders are probably best served by keeping quiet and not dignifying the allegations with a response. In those instances a rebuttal can often make matters worse by sparking a very public debate that, in Ellis's words, feeds on itself. Each situation is different and complex, and leaders will need to weigh their options carefully before charting a course of action.

PERSONAL VERSUS PRIVATE

The more important issue regarding leadership that we can learn from the Hemings debate is that your private life does matter when it comes to how people perceive you as a leader. Jefferson attempted to compartmentalize his private and public life, to keep them separate, making sure that one had nothing to do with the other. He was insulted if reporters asked about his private affairs, and he refused to respond.

In theory it might be nice if people respected a leader's privacy. But in practice, most people (Americans especially) have shown no such inclination. The more powerful you are as a leader, the more people will be interested in your private life. The simple fact is that most people do care about what you do when you are away from the spotlight or out of the reach of the camera. People will take into account what you do offstage when it comes to assessing your character, your integrity, and your fitness to lead. That's part of the responsibility you must be willing to accept when you take on the mantle of leadership. You may not like it, but a degree of scrutiny is part and parcel of the responsibilities and rewards of the role.

Who you are as an individual, publicly and privately, really does matter. You will be judged as a whole person, not as a compartmentalized persona.

"A NEW EPOCH"

Perhaps the greatest success that came from Jefferson's first term as president was the Lewis and Clark expedition of 1804–1806. Many people are familiar with the magnificent journey of the two men and their team, known as the "Corps of Discovery." Less well known are the political maneuverings that went on behind the scenes—orchestrated by Jefferson in an impressive display of leadership—that led to the historic venture west.

In 1802 America learned that Spain had ceded the vast Louisiana Territory to France. That was bad news for America, because it meant that Napoleon and his army could now lay claim to the city of New Orleans, strategically positioned at the mouth of the Mississippi River. Jefferson wrote that "there is on the globe one single spot, the possessor of which is our natural and habitual enemy. It is New Orleans, through which the produce of three-eighths of our territory must pass to market. . . . France placing herself in that door assumes to us the attitude of defiance."

Jefferson recognized that the presence of European forces in the American West, be they English or French, would threaten the stability and limit the promise of the United States. He wrote the ambassador to France, Robert Livingston, that he was most concerned about the situation, "so deep an impression it makes in my mind. It completely reverses all the political relations of the U.S. and will form a new epoch in our political course."

The changing geopolitical scene might drive the United States to seek a military alliance with the British for help against a French invasion—a course of action Jefferson very reluctantly considered. "This is not a state of things we seek or desire," he wrote. "We shall so take our distance between the two rival nations, as, remaining disengaged till necessity compels us, we may haul finally to the enemy of that which shall make it necessary." Since Napoleon seemed intent on sending an army to assume control of New Orleans and the Mississippi, the President and his advisors discussed the prospects of war.

"CORPS OF DISCOVERY"

Jefferson hoped that negotiations to purchase the territory from France would avoid any chance of violence between the nations. Joseph Ellis writes that

> though eminently capable, Livingston possessed the singular disadvantage of not being a Virginian. Jefferson wanted someone on the ground in Paris whom he could trust implicitly. So he in effect ordered James Monroe, a Jefferson protégé currently serving as governor of Virginia, to become a special envoy to France. Monroe was authorized to purchase New Orleans and as much of the Mississippi Valley as possible for up to $10 million—even the paramount domestic goal of

debt reduction was subordinate to recovering control over America's interior.

Hamilton and the Federalists, not confident in diplomatic efforts alone, urgently called for war and suggested that Jefferson send troops to take New Orleans. But the President remained calm and focused on his peaceful strategy. He had great faith in diplomacy—some would say too much, but in this case it proved to be the right course. Facing a war with Britain for which he needed financing, Napoleon offered to sell not only New Orleans but the entire Louisiana Territory for roughly $15 million. Jefferson jumped at the chance to buy it. In the best-known real estate deal in American history, the country more than doubled in size.

It was during the tense period of uncertain negotiations with France that Jefferson conceived of an expedition to investigate the West. With support from Congress, Jefferson sent his personal secretary, Meriwether Lewis, and army officer William Clark to explore the territories west of the Mississippi River. The Corps of Discovery team spent over two years traveling and recording their discoveries. Their journals of the mission are some of the most captivating reading in the history of American literature.

"IT IS INCUMBENT"

Though he had managed to avert war while increasing the land holdings of the country, Jefferson was denounced by some of his opponents for his part in the deal. His critics charged that he had essentially violated his own principles of a restrained government to buy the Louisiana Territory. In his own written response to those criticisms, Jefferson underscored an important principle of national leadership that he had learned as president.

A strict observance of the written laws is doubtless one of the high duties of a good citizen, but it is not the highest. The laws of necessity, of self-preservation, of saving our country when in danger, are of higher obligation. To lose our country by a scrupulous adherence to written law would be to lose the law itself, with life, liberty, property and all those who are enjoying them with us; thus absurdly sacrificing the end to the means. . . . It is incumbent on those only who accept of great charges, to risk themselves on great occasions, when the safety of the nation or some of its very high interests are at stake.

LEADERSHIP AND THE LOUISIANA PURCHASE

There are five important lessons of leadership that Thomas Jefferson demonstrated in purchasing the Louisiana Territory from France.

1. Don't Rush into Battle

Be wary of confrontations for which you might not be prepared. Check your emotions and consider your options with a thoughtful logic. Exhaust every effort at diplomatic negotiation before you commit to battle.

2. Send Representatives You Trust

Above all else, trust is the critical factor when it comes to selecting individuals who will represent you at the negotiating table. You should be able to anticipate their actions and reactions in any situation. Know these people extraordinarily well.

3. Learn Your Opponent's Needs

Make a detailed assessment of your opponent's immediate needs and challenges. Be prepared to take as much of an advantage as possible from these findings. Napoleon needed money fast to fund a war against Britain, and Jefferson was ready to take advantage of that.

4. Discover the Unknown

Invest in efforts to explore and map territories that may be to you unknown. Cultivate a Corps of Discovery attitude among those you lead, encouraging them to work as teams to seek out new ideas and map uncharted regions.

5. Dare to Risk Yourself on Great Occasions

Most important, remember the "higher obligations" and principles that guide you. Be willing to risk your leadership and legacy in support of those principles, even if that means abandoning written rules and procedures.

"WAR IS NOT THE BEST ENGINE"

Most Americans approved of Jefferson's actions when they learned of the Louisiana Purchase. News of the successful deal helped to stifle the Hemings controversy and to propel the President into a second term in 1804. But the second would not end on as triumphant a note as the first.

War plagued his second term. The battles between Britain and France were causing immense problems for Americans. Since the United States had not taken sides in the war, U.S. merchant ships were violently seized by the navies of both countries. Jefferson was faced with a decision, as scholar and author Robert Johnstone explains:

> The dilemma for Jefferson was to select a policy from alternative strategies no one of which was intrinsically desirable. There were as he saw it four options from which to choose should the belligerents fail to alter their courses. The choice of war was fraught with the obvious perils of waste, destruction, and possible defeat, but the real problem was deciding which country to fight, Britain or France, or horror of horrors both at once. To wage a successful war simultaneously against the greatest land power and the greatest sea power in the world was out of the question. The second and third alternatives were related and equally risky: the use of warships to protect American commerce or the arming of merchant vessels to the same purpose—would risk a war by default, provoke a war. The fourth option then, an embargo on all commercial intercourse with the offending nation or nations, appeared increasingly to be the most feasible solution.

Hoping once again to steer the country away from the threat of war, Jefferson and his supporters in Congress passed an Embargo Act in December 1807. The new law ordered every American port closed to all but domestic trade. The official policy of the administration was one of economic coercion, not armed conflict. Jefferson called the embargo "the last card we have to play, short of war." He wrote to John Langdon, the governor of New Hampshire, "I think one war enough for the life of one man; and you and I have gone through one which at least may lessen our impatience to embark in another." Every effort would be made to "avoid if possible wasting the energies of our people in war and destruction." In another letter the President said,

War is not the best engine for us to resort to, nature has given us one in our commerce, which, if properly managed, will be a better instrument for obliging the interested nations of Europe to treat us with justice.

"BITTERLY ATTACKED"

But the embargo was nearly impossible to enforce, and commercial interests up and down the coast, unwilling to lose profits, violated the new law. Jefferson was forced to sign additional measures that gave the federal government the authority to take control of all trading. Ports were slammed shut.

The net effect shattered the economy. Thirty thousand seamen lost their jobs. Historian Wendell Garrett notes that American merchants resorted to illegal smuggling: "Small businesses and the little folk—farmers, traders, and artisans—were hit severely and became the chief sufferers of Jefferson's measures. Ports were idle, ships dismantled, bankruptcies multiplied, and discontent spread." Garrett concludes that "at no time during [Jefferson's] long political career were his motives less partisan and more zealously nationalistic; at no time either was he more bitterly attacked."

Just days before he stepped down at the end of his second term as president in 1809, Jefferson signed an order repealing the Embargo Act. He had overestimated the degree to which England and France would be influenced by it, and he had grossly underestimated the detrimental effects it might have on his own country. It was a bold move, but it was widely noted as a failure. James Madison, who succeeded Jefferson in the White House, had little choice left but to lead the country into war against England. Willing now to admit that a war was unavoidable, Jefferson supported that decision.

Given the alternatives he had to select from, Jefferson probably opted for the best possible course of action. It was commendable that he did not launch the country into a war without trying every diplomatic means to avoid it. To his credit, he did manage to put off hostilities for which the country was certainly not prepared.

Leadership is fraught with difficult decisions. Even though you have weighed the pros and cons of each possible course of action and have chosen the one that makes most sense, given the circumstances, that does not mean your plan will necessarily meet the kind of success you envisioned. It might enjoy a limited success or can perhaps fail miserably. Leaders prepare themselves for any outcome by being ready to reevaluate their tactics and reconsider a new plan as situations develop and consequences become clearer.

Jefferson the President: Some Final Thoughts

After four decades of life as a public leader, Thomas Jefferson definitely knew what it felt like to win, to achieve great success, to be praised by his country. He also knew firsthand what it felt like to lose, to fail, to be criticized and denounced. His extraordinary career demonstrates a fundamental law of leadership: Challenges and difficulties will never disappear. There will always be a new obstacle around the corner. Such will be the case whether you are the president of a school club or of the United States. Effective leaders are those who accept that adventure and meet adversity head-on, willingly, with excitement and determination. Your success as a leader will come as much from your ability to win as from your capacity to persevere when you have lost.

- Your priority when accepting a position of authority over others should be to immediately spell out the standards by which your leadership will be measured. Be the one to create the criteria.

- Do not be wary of speaking in general terms. When used with integrity, it can be a powerful way to express your vision and motivate others to join your cause.
- Convincing messages can be sent without ever saying a word. Learn to use symbolism to your advantage. Appreciate rituals and customs that have deep meaning for others.
- Win with grace—be humble, conciliatory, and make an appeal to reason, moderation, and cooperation.
- Real leaders bury the hatchet and invite opposing forces to join them in working for the greater good.
- When choosing your team, select capable people whom you trust or who bolster your leadership. Use staff to compensate for your weaknesses.
- Successful management is fluid, indirect, informal, and ultimately based on the empowerment of others. With pragmatism as your guide, give people the room to use their abilities and fulfill their promise.
- Make an effort to bring people together in an informal and relaxed setting. You can often accomplish a great deal by seeing that business is done "more easily and more amicably."
- When talking with others, your goal should be to put the spotlight on them and make them feel special. Be the consummate facilitator.
- When it comes to assessing your character, your integrity, and your legacy, your private life does matter.
- No matter the emotion of the moment, don't rush into battles for which you might not be prepared.
- Choose representatives you trust implicitly.
- Assess your opponent's immediate needs and take advantage of them.

- Encourage a Corps of Discovery attitude, inspiring subordinates with the courage and tenacity to act as teams, mapping uncharted regions and exploring new ideas in their fields.
- Be willing to risk yourself on great occasions in support of fundamental principles and higher obligations.
- Leaders prepare themselves for any outcome by being ready to reevaluate their tactics and reconsider a new plan.

CHAPTER 10

JEFFERSON THE EDUCATOR

This institution of my native state, the hobby of my old age, will be based on the illimitable freedom of the human mind, to explore and to expose every subject susceptible of its contemplation.

Thomas Jefferson returned to Monticello in March 1809, having remained in Washington just long enough to attend the presidential inauguration of his friend James Madison. During the last eight hours of the 125-mile journey back to Charlottesville, Jefferson struggled through a terrible snowstorm to reach his mountaintop home. He endured the elements—just as he had labored through the responsibility of public life for many years—to reach that much-anticipated retirement for which he had so longed.

Shortly before he left the White House Jefferson had written, "Never did a prisoner released from his chains feel such relief as I shall on shaking off the shackles of power. Nature intended me for the tranquil pursuits of science, by rendering them my supreme delight. But the enormities of the time in which I have lived have forced me to take a part in resisting them, and to commit myself on the boisterous ocean of political passions."

If ever there was a man ready for retirement it was Jefferson, who was just shy of his sixty-sixth birthday when he left the White House. After four decades of public service he seemed to want nothing more than to spend the remaining years of his life doing the things he enjoyed most—reading, writing letters, playing with his grandchildren, gardening, and riding his horse across the countryside he had known since he was a small boy. He good-humoredly referred to himself in one letter as the "hermit of Monticello." But as many retirees have found, his quiet years were often anything but tranquil.

Well-wishers frequently climbed the mountain to Monticello to meet the great leader in his retirement. Some of these callers pressed their faces to the windows to watch him eating, strolled through the front door unannounced, and even made off with bits and pieces of Monticello as mementos.

He was bombarded with letters, more than one hundred a month, from old friends, acquaintances, and strangers—all of whom he felt he should answer personally. The time he took each morning to answer the letters kept getting longer and became nearly unbearable when his hands were gripped by arthritis. The management of his five-thousand-acre estate was no small task, and Jefferson found it difficult to turn a profit from his many fields. Ex-presidents at that time did not receive a pension, so he was dependent on the money he could earn from farming. In 1815 he was forced to sell his precious library of sixty-five hundred volumes to the federal government to get enough money to pay some of his debts. That collection became the foundation for the Library of Congress.

During this period Thomas Jefferson also took time to renew his friendship with fellow patriot John Adams. Jefferson and Adams had not spoken for over a decade, separated by political strife and partisan bickering. Their friendship picked up where it had left off, and their correspondence survives as one of the most important in the history of American letters.

Though in his mid-seventies and finally enjoying the retirement he had long sought, Jefferson embarked on what would prove to be both a challenging and rewarding project, founding the University of Virginia. No other subject occupied his time more during these years than this monumental endeavor, which began in earnest in 1817.

"A YOUNG GARDENER"

Along with reading and architecture, Jefferson's favorite activity was gardening. But not until his final retirement did he at last have the free time to devote to cultivating the vegetables, fruits, and flowers that so fascinated him. When he returned to Monticello in 1809 Jefferson took up gardening with youthful enthusiasm. He spent hours in the fields aligning lettuce rows, examining the latest peach crop, and designing the arrangement of flower beds. Jefferson wrote,

> I have often thought that if heaven had given me choice of my position and calling, it should have been on a rich spot of earth, well watered, and near a good market for the productions of the garden. No occupation is so delightful to me as the culture of the earth, and no culture comparable to that of the garden. But though an old man, I am but a young gardener.

With the assistance and labor of his talented gardener, Wormley, and other enslaved African Americans, Jefferson created a thousand-foot-long garden terrace on the side of the mountain below Monticello. Here he grew hundreds of varieties of vegetables. While not a vegetarian, Thomas Jefferson ate little red meat. He preferred that vegetables be the primary emphasis of each meal and that meat be served as a complementary side dish. Most of what appeared on the table in his dining room came from these very gardens.

Monticello's fruit garden, or "fruitery," as Jefferson called it, included an eight-acre field with hundreds of trees—apples, peaches, and cherries among them. He had planted an extensive vineyard and plots of berry patches that offered figs, currants, and raspberries. The flower gardens that lined the roads and walkways on the mountain were laden with hyacinths, tulips, irises, and a host of other species; their blooming seasons marked off the passing months like a natural calendar.

Jefferson followed the progress of everything that grew in his garden. He watched with enchantment as the landscape came alive around him with color and sustenance. During his retirement he especially enjoyed walking in the vegetable garden in the shady cool of the evening, pulling weeds and plucking tomatoes from the vines.

"THE CHOSEN PEOPLE"

Working the soil was much more than just a relaxing pastime for Jefferson. Despite all his other accomplishments he considered his chief occupation throughout his life to be simply that of an Albemarle County farmer. While that may smack of political rhetoric, which it probably was to a certain degree, there was some truth to it. Leaving the White House and taking up the hoe in his vegetable garden was to him a joyous step closer to his true pleasures. A part of him seems to have truly believed that he was nothing more than a gardener.

Jefferson kept incredibly detailed records of his efforts—his now famous farm and garden books—in which he noted and tracked the progress of his gardens as scientists would their latest experiments. For Jefferson, agriculture was the greatest science of all. It brought together in one pursuit the intellectual and spiritual aspects of life. It was both a true science and a moral blessing to labor in the earth. He admired the efforts of a talented gardener, and held farmers in high regard. As Jefferson had noted in 1781,

> Those who labor in the earth are the chosen people of God, if ever He had a chosen people, whose breasts he has made his peculiar deposit for substantial and genuine virtue. It is the focus in which He keeps alive that sacred fire which otherwise might escape from the face of the earth.

"MOST TRANQUIL, HEALTHY, AND INDEPENDENT"

Farming and gardening were to Thomas Jefferson the ideal vocations of all Americans. His vision for the United States was a coast-to-coast version of Albemarle County—he called it "Virginia-writ-large." It would be a society of industrious farmers, each with his own plot of land—self-sufficient, self-reliant, moving to the rhythms of the natural world. It was also inherently communal, as many farmers depended on their neighbors for assistance from time to time. For Jefferson, such a scenario meant that each citizen could be largely independent and yet still tied to their families and communities.

This vision might appear a bit naïve, especially coming from a man who served as president during the dawn of the Industrial Revolution. And there is, of course, the degree to which many "self-sufficient" farmers actually depended for their livelihood on slave labor. But the essential point is this: Jefferson believed that agriculture would be for the American citizen "the most tranquil, healthy, and independent occupation." He once wrote to Madison,

> I think our governments will remain virtuous for many centuries; as long as they are chiefly agricultural; and this will be as long as there shall be vacant lands in any part of America. When they get piled upon one another in large cities, as in Europe, they will become corrupt as in Europe.

In Jefferson's view, growing vegetables and fruits, tending crops, or nurturing a bed of flowers offered people a priceless experience they weren't going to find in the confines of a factory.

The perennial lessons of the earth—unaffected yet powerful precepts that any gardener knows—comprised a tapestry of knowledge that Jefferson held was necessary learning for all Americans. He even suggested that gardening should be joined with architecture, painting, sculpture, and music as a required course of study for students.

In Jefferson's vision, America was a nation of leaders—self-governing individuals, each entrusted with the responsibility and care of the country's well-being. Farmers, gardeners, and all those who work with the earth were uniquely qualified to serve in this democratic role because they each—by the nature of their work—had a clear understanding of the essential principles of successful leadership. Here are ten of those principles, each a perennial lesson of the soil.

THE WISDOM OF A GARDENER

1. Get the Right Tools

Jefferson designed an improved moldboard to make plowing easier and more efficient. This achievement earned him a gold medal award from the French Society of Agriculture. Whether in farming, surveying, or in the pursuits of science, Jefferson clearly understood the value of having the right tools. No gardeners or farmers begin the growing season without first making sure that they have all the proper tools they will need to successfully make it through the year.

Likewise, leaders do not embark on a project without ensuring that the tools they will need are available and in good condition. That could possibly mean an improved computer system for your office or a new delivery truck for your small business. For someone else it could mean going back to school and getting advanced training in a specific field. Whatever it is, make sure you have the right tools to begin the work you want to do.

2. *Prepare the Ground*

"When earth is rich," Jefferson observed in the summer of 1793, "it bids defiance to droughts, yields in abundance and of the best quality." The initial step in creating a productive garden is to carefully select the ground where you want to work, then to enrich that soil with the right balance of nutrients.

For great leaders this means focusing your efforts. Decide first where you want to concentrate your skills. Where will your garden be this season? As the head of a company, for example, you could imagine your garden in any number of departments—customer service, research and development, sales, or a new Internet division. As the mayor of a town, you could plant your garden in an exciting new economic development project, in the school system, or in historic preservation and tourism. The key is to decide ahead of time where you will aim your efforts.

Jefferson did not create a vegetable garden by plowing one long row running down the side of his mountain. He cleverly designed a terrace cut into the side of the hill which would benefit from ample sunshine and collect rainwater that trickled down. Successful leaders must prepare their gardens with as much forethought and attention. Where is the ideal growing spot in your business? on your team? in your community?

3. Plow Deeply and Plant the Seed

During each growing season Jefferson was continually amazed at the abundance of life and color that arose from the tiniest seedlings. Great leaders know that no prosperous venture begins without first planting a small seed or germ of an idea with others. They know that great accomplishments can quite often come of seemingly insignificant beginnings. No true leader is dismissive of even the smallest suggestion or plan because there is no telling, given the right "soil," what that idea might one day produce.

When planting the seed, remember the Law of Plowing Deep. Jefferson wrote to a friend in 1814, "Plowing deep, your recipe for killing weeds, is also the recipe for almost every good thing in farming. The plow is to the farmer what the wand is to the sorcerer. Its effect is really like sorcery."

Though it may generate some initial excitement, a seed planted too close to the surface is weak and has little staying power. Its root system is shallow, and it is eventually strangled to death by weeds. But a seed planted deep enough produces a strong root system and promises to produce a vibrant plant that can overcome the weeds.

And so it is with leadership. If you want to see real growth, waste no time sowing shallow seeds. It will be quick, easy, and attract some hoopla, but it will not last or yield the results you are hoping for. An effective leader plants the seed of an idea or plan deep in the hearts of others, where their dreams, goals, and aspirations reside. That is the richest soil. We all have "weeds"—those daily concerns and stresses that get in our way and distract us from what is really important. But the seed of future action that is plowed deep in our hearts will take root, grow vigorously, and will survive despite the weeds of life.

4. Nurture the Seedling

Great leaders, like the best gardeners, know that any seed requires the utmost patience and care if it is to mature and bear fruit. Jefferson himself walked the rows of his vegetable and fruit garden every day, making sure that each fragile plant received the best care he could offer. He did not expect his efforts to produce baskets of tomatoes or peaches overnight. He knew that patient work would pay off at the harvest. Leaders take this same approach—exercising patience in all endeavors, nurturing and encouraging growth in all corners of their gardens.

5. Watch the Weather

Jefferson was one of the pioneers of American meteorology. Beginning in July 1776 and continuing until the last year of his life in 1826, he collected some of the most reliable weather reports in our country's history. He noted daily temperatures, rain- and snowfall amounts, and wind direction. Not only was Jefferson fascinated with weather as a scientific pursuit, but he also believed that the success of his gardens depended on how well he learned the natural patterns.

All leaders constantly "watch the weather." They keep an eye out for factors that will impact the progress and growth of their efforts. They look for patterns that might affect what goes on in their gardens. They are thinking ahead, scanning the skies for storms, always prepared.

6. Work the Day

Gardeners know all too well that no good crop will happen by itself. It takes hard work and a dedication to the growing process. The lesson for aspiring leaders is this: Don't be afraid to get down in the dirt or pick up a hoe when you need to. Be willing and ready to do the work that needs doing. Work the day; work the season; work the garden. Work your plan. Don't waste your efforts, and don't waste your time. In other words, make hay while the sun shines. In the end your efforts will be rewarded. As Pangloss remarks in the memorable closing scene of Voltaire's *Candide*: "When man was put in the Garden of Eden, he was put there to dress it and to keep it, that is, to work; which proves that man was not born to be idle."

7. Weed and Prune

Not everything that grows in the garden is welcome. Weeds will appear, unnecessary growth that has the potential to limit the success and vitality of your primary plants. Get rid of them so that you can stay focused on the growth that really matters. At the same time, gardeners do not hesitate to prune whenever the health of the plant will benefit in the long run. Snipping off a few leaves here and there allows the plant to concentrate on digging in deeper and strengthening its root system. Leaders know that weeding and pruning are natural aspects of any project. Weed out concerns and stresses that aren't good for the garden. And trim the plant now and then, cutting back in one place so that it has a chance to grow more in another.

8. Learn from the Best

Besides seeking out the advice and counsel of his neighbors in Charlottesville, Jefferson corresponded with Philadelphia nurseryman Bernard McMahon, perhaps the best-known and most-talented gardener of the period. Author of *The American Gardener*, a classic in early American horticulture, McMahon offered Jefferson excellent advice and suggestions for developing the gardens at Monticello. All wise leaders, even presidents and CEOs, seek the counsel of experts before making an important decision. They are humble enough to ask questions and to learn new things, no matter how much power and influence they may have.

9. Protect Your Garden

To protect his gardens and orchards from the deer, rabbits, and other wildlife that roamed the hills near Monticello, Jefferson had a ten-foot-high wooden fence constructed around the cultivated fields. The imposing stockade was almost a mile long. Impressive leaders likewise insulate their gardens from any negative influences. They work diligently to ensure that their team members feel safe and secure while they are bringing a project to life.

10. Celebrate Your Harvest

Jefferson rejoiced in the bounty of fruits and vegetables that were harvested from his gardens. He enjoyed sharing his produce with guests during meals, and often gave them as gifts. He loved to walk the garden paths at Monticello with his grandchildren, admiring the kaleidoscope of flowers that bloomed along the way. Take the time to celebrate your harvest. Rejoice in your accomplishments, and reward yourself and others for work well done. As you move forward in your accomplishments, remember to celebrate each passing victory. That will give you and your team encouragement and satisfaction, and make the next harvest all the more appealing.

WHAT ABOUT YOU?

Great leaders, like the best gardeners, are guided by these questions: Where will you set your garden this season? Have you prepared the soil? What fruit do you hope to produce? Do you have the right tools? Have you consulted the experts? Are you willing to be patient? to nurture the seedlings? to work each day? to weed and prune? Are you checking the weather? Have you devised a way to protect your efforts? And most important, Will you take time out to celebrate and reward yourself and your team when the harvest has arrived?

"VERY DEAR TO MY MIND"

We should consider briefly one particularly poignant episode from Jefferson's retirement years for the salient leadership lesson it offers. Thomas Jefferson and fellow patriot John Adams had once been firmly bound by friendship and a shared commitment to the total success of the American Revolution. They had worked alongside one another in the Continental Congress and as ambassadors to Europe. Adams publicly defended Jefferson's work as the Congress debated the particulars of the Declaration of Independence. And Jefferson similarly defended Adams on occasions when others thought him too irascible for public office.

But when Adams' Federalists and Jefferson's Democratic-Republicans engaged in open political warfare in Washington, their personal relationship suffered. Partisan bickering got the best of their mutual admiration, and their friendship collapsed altogether. They refused to talk or write to one another for over a decade. And they each bore their wounded egos and bruised sentiments into retirement.

Having left the politics of Washington behind and returned to Monticello, Jefferson beseeched a mutual friend, Dr. Benjamin Rush, to assist him in reconciling with Adams.

> With a man possessing so many other estimable qualities, why should we be dissocialized by mere differences of opinion in politics, in religion, in philosophy, or anything else? His opinions are as honestly formed as my own. Our different views of the same subject are the result of a difference in our organization and experience.

A few weeks later, with Jefferson's overtures of kindness communicated to him by Dr. Rush, Adams sat down and penned a letter of affection to his old friend. Jefferson received the letter in January 1812 and immediately responded in kind. "A letter from you calls up recollections very dear to my mind. It carries me back to the times when, beset with difficulties and dangers, we were fellow laborers in the same cause, struggling for what is most valuable to man, his right of self-government."

Their warm friendship resumed where it had left off years before and produced nearly 160 letters between them. In one moving exchange Jefferson wrote,

> I have thus stated my opinion on a point on which we differ, not with a view to controversy, for we are both too old to change opinions which are the result of a long life of inquiry and reflection, but on the suggestion of a former letter of yours that we ought not to die before we have explained ourselves to each other. We acted in perfect harmony through a long and perilous contest for our liberty and independence. A constitution has been acquired which, though neither of us think perfect, yet both consider as competent to render our fellow citizens the happiest and the securest on whom the sun has ever shone. If we do not think exactly alike as to its imperfections, it matters little to our country which, after devoting to it long lives of disinterested labor, we have delivered over to our successors in life, who will be able to take care of it and of themselves.

WHO IS YOUR ADAMS?

Life is much too short and often too trying to haul our bitter baggage and bruised egos around with us. It's just not worth it. Thomas Jefferson knew this. Despite their differences, he valued the friendship he had had with John Adams. Friends and colleagues can disagree on many things and still have a genuine and worthwhile bond. Instead of continuing to harp on what drove them apart, Jefferson and Adams focused on the common ground they shared.

Who is *your* John Adams? Who did you once count as an ally but with whom the tribulations of the day have somehow created a rift in your relationship? Who is it that you shared the struggles with but later found yourself divided from? A humble leader, following Jefferson's example, takes the initiative to craft a sincere reconciliation, whether it is with a family member, an old friend, a co-worker, or a teammate. Clear a space on peaceful, common ground, and invite them to join you there. There is so much more that can be accomplished when the bitter baggage has at last been set down.

"FREEDOM AND HAPPINESS"

Certainly one of the episodes that most showcases Jefferson's leadership came late in his life. The founding of the University of Virginia stands as one of his most impressive and celebrated accomplishments. A landmark in the history of education in America, the university was ahead of its time in many respects. The culmination of a lifelong dream for Jefferson, it stands as a hallmark to his ingenuity, perseverance, and vision.

During his retirement Jefferson took time between writing letters, gardening, and riding his horse, Eagle, around the countryside, to entertain the intellectual queries of young men and boys living in Charlottesville. In 1810 he commented that "they place themselves in the neighborhood and have the use of my library and counsel and make a part of my society. In advising the course of their reading, I endeavor to keep their attention fixed on the main objects of all science, the freedom and happiness of man."

Education was of course the key to making a democratic republic succeed. If a free society hoped to survive the inevitable power grab of wealthy oligarchs, every one of its members had to be literate and educated enough to participate in the decision-making process that citizens in a democracy can enjoy. Education was therefore not just important to Jefferson personally; it was an absolutely critical ingredient to the success of the fragile republic he had helped to create.

In the process of founding the University of Virginia, Jefferson made excellent use of the leadership skills and techniques that he had mastered over the course of his lifetime.

BELIEVE IN YOUR VISION

It wasn't just any kind of education Jefferson had in mind. Like his ideas on self-government and freedom of expression, his thoughts on schooling were truly revolutionary. Jefferson dreamed of public schools throughout the country that were free from the religious creeds and interference of the church. He wanted to see schools that operated without any obligation to maintain a particular religious doctrine.

Throughout his life Jefferson never gave up on this dream and consistently advocated programs that would implement progressive public education in America. As a Virginia legislator he introduced the state's very first education bill. The measure, if it had passed, would have created a state-supported three-level educational system made up of elementary and secondary schools, and a statewide university. Though the act failed at first in the General Assembly, Jefferson's formula has since become standard practice around the United States.

As governor, Jefferson attempted to make sweeping reforms at his alma mater, the College of William and Mary. Always steadfast in his belief in maintaining a separation between church and state, he had hoped to loosen the grip that the clergy had on the school. He wanted to open up the teaching posts to secular scholars and to broaden the curriculum. But his plans were aggressively opposed by many Virginia conservatives and were ultimately defeated. During his presidency Jefferson made an effort to establish a national university to be located in Virginia—a project originally championed by Washington. But those plans fell through when support waned as debate over the site intensified.

In his retirement Jefferson continued to promote his vision of a public-sponsored school system in America. In 1810 he penned a bill that helped create a state literary fund in Virginia, from which future education projects could be financed. If enough money could be set aside ahead of time, he reasoned, perhaps the legislators would be more likely in the future to invest in education. This approach eventually succeeded, as the money from the fund was later used to create the University of Virginia in Charlottesville.

In these pursuits we again witness Jefferson's remarkable persistence. Establishing an educational program in Virginia—a visionary archetype that would serve as a model for the rest of the nation—was a dream he sought to realize for decades. The revolution was not fulfilled, he believed, until a progressive system of public education was in place. Until excellent schools with qualified teachers were within the reach of children around the country, all of them potential leaders for the future, our liberties were on shaky ground. Jefferson held fast to this dream and doggedly pursued it even into his retirement years. An exemplary leader, he was tenacious and uncompromising in his vision. He was willing to keep up the fight for his ideal public schools even though his proposals were soundly defeated for decades.

He faced powerful adversaries: Political conservatives and influential members of the clergy were not shy about opposing his revolutionary approach to education. They attacked him as a dangerous liberal, but Jefferson was unwavering in his determination. He continued to believe in the possibilities of his dream despite the naysayers who told him it would never work. After a lifetime of trying, his perseverance paid off.

SEE IT BIG

In the spring of 1814 Jefferson joined his nephew Peter Carr and other area landowners at the Old Stone Tavern in Charlottesville. The purpose of this meeting was to discuss plans for starting a local secondary school, then being called the Albemarle Academy. Carr and the others had asked Jefferson to join them at the meeting, well aware that he had always been an advocate of public education and that he might be able to offer them some sound advice about establishing a school.

Still carrying his vision of the ideal state university, Jefferson was more than willing to offer his input. But he urged the men to think bigger—imagine something greater than just a local high school. He told his neighbors that they had a tremendous opportunity to create a university for the entire state of Virginia. In this Jefferson exemplified one of the hallmark principles of effective leadership. He shared a vision for the future and called others to join him on that exciting path. He dared the trustees of the Albemarle Academy to think of a grander plan.

Leaders invite us to imagine greater goals and to stretch ourselves beyond what we think we can achieve. They challenge our limitations and inspire us to do more.

Here at last, years into his retirement, he saw a way to realize the dream he had pursued for so long. But he could not accomplish the project by himself. He would need allies and supporters. And he had to go further by convincing his adversaries that his plan was a good investment for the state. The same courage and vision that almost forty years earlier drove the young man who wrote the Declaration of Independence now fueled the seventy-one-year-old retiree.

Jefferson could have politely returned to Monticello and left the whole university scheme for a younger generation to worry about. He could have told Peter Carr and the others that he was retired now and not interested in getting involved in another project that took a lot of time. He was suffering from the disabilities of old age and from financial concerns. It would have been extremely easy to retreat to his vegetable garden. But Jefferson was not that type of leader. Instead he threw himself into the fray once again, daring to achieve one last fantastic dream.

BUILD YOUR TEAM WITH WELL-PLACED ALLIES AND PEOPLE YOU TRUST

Jefferson's first step toward founding the University of Virginia was to establish a new and more powerful board of trustees. The original group comprised of Albemarle County planters—while well known in central Virginia—did not alone have the political connections and experience to put together something as magnificent as he had in mind.

Jefferson called on his disciples and fellow Virginians James Madison and James Monroe. Madison was just wrapping up his second term as president of the United States and Monroe was on his way into the White House. Both were encouraged and inspired by Jefferson's interest in planning a state university and willingly offered their assistance.

Jefferson also called on two close allies who would prove to have significant roles in the success of the project, Joseph Carrington Cabell and John Hartwell Cocke. As Jefferson's point man in the General Assembly in Richmond, Cabell was instrumental in communicating the vision and grandeur of Jefferson's plans to the other state legislators. He lobbied for Jefferson's university with a fiery passion. Cocke personally helped Jefferson oversee much of the day-to-day work that had to be done and remained dedicated to the University of Virginia well after Jefferson's death.

All four of the men handpicked by Jefferson to join him in this historic venture of creating an unprecedented school on American soil had already proven themselves. Jefferson knew beyond a doubt that he could trust them to fight for his vision. And he believed they had the abilities and skills to succeed.

WORK THE PLAN

Thomas Jefferson was there at every important step along the way toward founding the University of Virginia. He committed his talents and experience to realizing the goal, and he diligently worked and reworked his plans. With his team in place Jefferson solicited the favor of the governor and state legislators who would ultimately make the decision about where to locate Virginia's university. The debate had already begun, and various local interests were vying for the honor. Supporters and alumni of the College of William and Mary were seeking to have their school selected as the university, as were organizers for a site in Richmond and representatives of Washington College (later Washington and Lee University) in the Shenandoah Valley.

Mindful that the Virginia legislature was looking for a central location in which to open a state school, Jefferson cleverly renamed his project "Central College" in early 1816. He personally selected a site for the school, an empty field at the crest of a ridge about a mile west of Charlottesville, on land that had once been a farm owned by James Monroe. The land, though it wasn't his first choice, commanded an awe-inspiring view of the mountains and included plenty of fresh springs and ponds.

Jefferson began work on designing the school. He patterned the plan after a New England village, with professors and students housed together in one intimate community arranged around a wide green lawn. He called it an "Academical Village." The cornerstone of the first building, Pavilion Seven, was laid on October 6, 1817.

Jefferson's approach to winning the charter for the state university was similar to the approach a city might take today to garner a new team franchise from the National Football League. Supporters of such a bid begin by spending millions to build a stadium, sell season tickets, select a name for the team, and set up marketing contracts. In other words, they go ahead and commit to the project even before they earn the franchise. They demonstrate the lengths to which they are willing to go to earn the privilege of hosting a team.

Jefferson exhibited the same confident leadership in creating his ideal school. He personally designed the plans and facilities for the school, oversaw fund-raising efforts, selected the books for the library, developed a curriculum, hired the teachers, and daily supervised construction of the buildings. Only then, when things were well under way and his commitment to the project was evident to all, he earnestly solicited the charter that would transform Central College into the University of Virginia.

After more debate and heated arguments in the General Assembly, Jefferson's efforts were rewarded when his college received the state charter in January 1819. The University of Virginia was born. Thomas Jefferson's dream for progressive education in America was a reality. Historian Clay Jenkinson has commented that

> Jefferson saw this as a hobby in his old age but I think its purpose was much more serious than that. He was afraid that the revolutionary edge of the founding generation would not be recapitulated in the younger generation. And so he wanted to create a temple to the Enlightenment in his old age—and he did.

STAY COMMITTED TO YOUR VISION

Against the wishes of many people around the state, Jefferson declared that none of the professors at the university would be members of the clergy and that the school would take no position to support one religion over another. He further mandated, following his theme of self-government, that the University of Virginia would have no bureaucratic controls other than a Board of Visitors. There would be no university president. The professors and students would work together to run the school themselves. The members of the academic community, like the citizens of the United States, would each be called upon to assume positions of leadership and do their parts to govern.

In December 1820 Jefferson joyously wrote that "this institution of my native state, the hobby of my old age, will be based on the illimitable freedom of the human mind, to explore and to expose every subject susceptible of its contemplation." In another letter the following day he added the now oft-quoted description of the school: "For here we are not afraid to follow truth wherever it may lead, nor to tolerate any error so long as reason is left free to combat it."

Jefferson tended the University as he did his gardens, with a daily vigilance and unwavering care. He rode out to the school each day to check on the progress of its buildings. No element of the project escaped his influence.

After decades of service in public life—during which he frequently doubted the results of his efforts—Jefferson at last felt that his work on founding the University of Virginia would be of some good. It was his sincere wish that he would live long enough to see the University open to students. "It is the last act of usefulness I can render," he wrote in March 1821, "and could I see it open I would not ask an hour more of life."

The University of Virginia opened its doors to students in March 1825, and eighty-three-year-old Thomas Jefferson was there to welcome the first class. He enjoyed visiting the University in its first year and often hosted students for dinner at Monticello.

"IS IT THE FOURTH?"

Jefferson made his last visit to the University of Virginia in June 1826. After meeting with the librarian to discuss the classification of some new books, he walked slowly up the Lawn to the Rotunda. There he sat for over an hour by himself at the second-floor window, watching students and professors walk back and forth to their classes. In the distance the plum-colored peaks of the Ragged Mountains reached to the horizon.

We can only imagine the sense of accomplishment he must have felt at that moment. He had finally realized his dream of a university free of church dogma (the first of its kind in the world), ready to educate and inspire the leaders of a new nation. Thomas Jefferson's University of Virginia is today recognized as the top public university in America. It has produced countless alumni who have gone on to assume leadership positions in government, business, the arts, sports, and in schools and communities around the world. Jefferson would be proud indeed.

A few days after his last visit to the University, Jefferson was bedridden with severe intestinal pain. Historians believe he was probably suffering from colon or prostate cancer and possibly diabetes. For some time he had taken daily drops of opium to fight the pain, but those were no longer doing any good. Jefferson's physician and friend, Robley Dunglison, was called to Monticello, where he found the old man propped up in his small bed.

Sunday night, July 2, Thomas Jefferson drifted into a deep sleep. Dr. Dunglison later remembered his final hours:

> About seven o'clock of the evening of the 3rd of July he awoke, and seeing me staying at his bedside exclaimed, "Ah Doctor, are you still there?" in a voice however that was husky and indistinct. He then asked, "Is it the fourth?" to which I replied, "It soon will be." These were the last words I heard him utter. He died at 12 o'clock and 50 minutes on July 4, having remained all that day wholly unconscious to everything around him.

Thomas Jefferson died on a Tuesday afternoon, July 4, 1826—the fiftieth anniversary of the Declaration of Independence. Just a few hours later, at his home in Quincy, Massachusetts, John Adams passed away as well.

Two days later Jefferson was laid to rest in the family graveyard at Monticello. As per Jefferson's instructions, the site was marked with a granite obelisk inscribed with the following epitaph:

"Thomas Jefferson, Author of the Declaration of American Independence, of the Statute of Virginia for Religious Freedom, and Father of the University of Virginia."

Jefferson the Educator: Some Final Thoughts

No matter how accomplished, a great leader is one who is always working toward new goals and bigger dreams. No one illustrates that principle more than Jefferson in his drive to found the University of Virginia in his old age. Leadership means being ready at all times to heed the call of adventure and challenge—even when you least expect it.

Retired, with his family, books, and gardens to take up his time, Jefferson could easily have foregone the invitation to participate in creating an outstanding university in Charlottesville. To the benefit of many generations of men and women, he chose the more difficult path. He was willing to chase down that dream, and America is the better for it.

What is your University of Virginia? What is the ambitious, visionary project you have been nurturing that is still unfulfilled? Thomas Jefferson has shown us all that it is never too late to pursue a dream. To make real your vision you will need a plan of action, allies and supporters you can trust, a vision of your success, and a willingness to dedicate yourself to the process despite all opposition. Your call to adventure may come when you least expect it. Be ready.

- Great leaders know the Perennial Lessons of the Soil—prepare the ground well; plant a seed in deeply plowed soil; use the right tools; nurture the seedling; watch the weather; make hay when the sun shines; weed and prune;

consult the experts; protect your efforts; and celebrate your harvest.

- Who is your John Adams? Leadership means taking responsibility in one's personal life to mend relationships and end old disputes. Nothing is gained by hauling bitter baggage through your life.
- The value of well-placed allies cannot be underestimated. Make sure your allies know that you consider them a part of your team and that you appreciate their efforts.
- See it big! Leaders call us to imagine grander goals and to stretch ourselves beyond that which we think we can achieve.
- What is your University of Virginia? What is the ambitious goal or project of your life that remains undone? It's never too late to begin a new adventure.

THE FINAL CHALLENGE

The boisterous sea of liberty is never without a wave.

In his award-winning study of the character of Thomas Jefferson, *American Sphinx,* historian Joseph Ellis writes that "different versions of him as both hero and villain are loose among us, and different claims on the Jeffersonian legacy have become a permanent feature of contemporary American culture." Jefferson can be "all things to all people."

The nature of his legacy will long continue to be a source of debate and discussion, as well it should be. For when we contemplate the influence, character, and philosophy of Thomas Jefferson, we come face-to-face with the paradox at the heart of the American experience—how do we reconcile the ideals of individual freedom, human equality, justice, and the pursuit of happiness? They are not always and in every circumstance mutually compatible.

For many people Jefferson is the apostle of democratic liberty—his inspiring prose and extraordinary life offer illumination at every turn. For others he is the ultimate symbol of America's ability to screen injustice and inequality behind a veil of eloquent rhetoric that sings the promises of progress. Either way, we can agree that Jefferson provides us ample fodder to consider improvements in our own lives.

Key themes have emerged as we have considered his life from the perspective of leadership—an emphasis on self-improvement, education, and responsibility; an enduring faith that human beings have the capacity to do great things with their lives if they are given the motivation, opportunity, and freedom to succeed; a belief in character, merit, and talent over wealth and privilege; an unwavering optimism for the prospects of a democratic society; an understanding that effective leadership means empowering others; and a decidedly practical approach to opportunities and challenges.

Jefferson's pragmatism teaches us to remain absolutely fixed on the goals we have set before us as a free people. But we should remember that those goals are not good government or even less government; compassionate conservatism or enlightened liberalism; bipartisanship, profitable industries, peace in the streets, or democracy itself. No, those are not the goals.

Our goal as a free people is the preservation and strengthening of individual human liberties—protecting everyone's inalienable rights to life, liberty, and the pursuit of happiness. All else—government, business, or the law—is just a collection of tools we have developed to help us achieve those ends. And as Jefferson so wisely cautioned us, we must not confuse the two or sacrifice the end to the means.

Perhaps the most important thing we can learn by considering the life and leadership of Thomas Jefferson is that the battle against tyranny, corruption, and injustice is never finished. Jefferson was an ardent student of history, and he had a firm grasp on the realities of power in society. He understood that "the natural progress of things is for liberty to yield and government to gain ground"—and not just government, but any human institution that profits from the suppression of self-rule and civil liberties.

Circumstances of history present every generation with new challenges that demand a reinvigorated commitment to the preservation of liberty and the cultivation of inspired individuals to lead the fight. Leadership is no academic enterprise. Freedom is never a guarantee.

At the start of the American Revolution, wealthy men could avoid the military draft by putting up money for substitutes to take their place. The poor on the other hand had no choice but to enlist and risk their lives. Historian Howard Zinn has written that this situation led to rioting in the streets of colonial America, where people were heard to shout: "Tyranny is tyranny, let it come from whom it may!"

Thomas Jefferson swore "upon the altar of God eternal hostility against every form of tyranny over the mind of man." In his own lifetime that meant risking everything to take on a government of aristocrats often guided by self-interest and not by the best interests of the majority of people. It meant going up against the Anglican church, which was intent on using the powers of state to extend its authority.

What about today? Where does tyranny take shape in our own time? There are some people who identify it precisely where Jefferson did two hundred years ago—in an indulgent government dominated by the interests of the rich and powerful, or among religious institutions who seek to exert undue political influence.

Others find tyranny in an activist judiciary, in the commercial media, or in the militarization of law enforcement. Still others see it in the globalization of mammoth corporations that wield unprecedented power throughout the world, putting private profits ahead of democracy in the name of "free trade." Tyranny has the potential to exist wherever the door to democracy is slammed shut, where the fundamentals of liberty are subjugated to concerns of profit and power, and whenever consumerism becomes more important than citizenship.

No matter where people take their stand against the autocratic tendencies of any institution, Thomas Jefferson is there to inspire their mission. The positive aspects of the legacy of his leadership teach us never to be complacent when the principles of democracy are at stake. As global justice activist Sarah Blackstock has written,

> The struggle is about insisting that democracy is more than regular, well-managed elections where citizens choose representatives from among a narrow group of like-minded elites. Democracy is about self-rule. It's about people participating in the political activity and decisions that affect our lives. It's recognizing that neither politicians nor a faceless market drive society. It is people—our work and ideas—who create the kinds of worlds we live in.

Inspired by Jefferson's leadership, courageous men and women will always stand at the ready, prepared to fight tyranny of any form, no matter from where or whom it may come. Acclaimed historian Rhys Isaac has commented that

> Jeffersonian principles stand as a perduring expression of the highest collective aspirations of the nation, while the confounding inequalities of his own and our present times remain a constant admonition that the revolutionary struggle is always to be kept up. It must be avowed that his predicament is still the nation's: the predicament of being enmeshed in forms of systematic injustice that seem forever to require radical redress.

MAKE THE DECISION

Before you set this book aside, find at least five principles of Jeffersonian leadership that apply to your life and your situation. Write them down on a piece of paper, and put that paper up where you can read it—taped to your bathroom mirror, for example, or on the visor of your car, the refrigerator, or on your wall at work. Read them aloud to yourself each and every day, and endeavor to bring those principles to life in all you do. Let the principles of leadership in this book be the tools to help you find your way, to forge your own path. You have heard the call to leadership. Your final challenge is to accept that call, to make the decision to be a leader, and to join the fight against every form of tyranny over the mind of humanity.

> *Some men look at constitutions with sanctimonious reverence, and deem them like the arc of the covenant, too sacred to be touched. They ascribe to the men of the preceding age a wisdom more than human, and suppose what they did to be beyond amendment. I knew that age well; I belonged to it, and labored with it. . . . Laws and institutions must go hand in hand with the progress of the human mind. As that becomes more developed, more enlightened, as new discoveries are made, new truths disclosed, and manners and opinions change with the change of circumstances, institutions must advance also, and keep pace with the times.*

> *If ever you find yourself environed with difficulties and perplexing circumstances out of which you are at a loss how to extricate yourself, do what is right, and be assured that that will extricate you the best out of the worst situations. Though you cannot see when you take one step what will be the next, yet follow truth, justice and plain dealing, and never fear their leading you out of the labyrinth in the easiest manner possible. . . . Be assured that nothing will be so pleasing as your success.*

FURTHER READING

This is certainly not a comprehensive list of available sources regarding the life and legacy of Thomas Jefferson, but is intended to provide possible starting points for those interested in continuing their study of Jefferson and related topics.

ORIGINAL WRITINGS

Papers of Thomas Jefferson: Julian P. Boyd et al., eds., 1950– .

Thomas Jefferson: Writings. Merrill D. Peterson, ed., 1984.

Jefferson's Literary Commonplace Book. Douglas L. Wilson, ed., 1989.

The Portable Thomas Jefferson. Merrill D. Peterson, ed., 1975; 1997.

BIOGRAPHIES

Jefferson Himself. Bernard Mayo, 1942; reprinted 1970.

Jefferson and His Time (six volumes). Dumas Malone,1948–81.

Thomas Jefferson and the New Nation. Merrill D. Peterson, 1970; reprinted 1987.

Thomas Jefferson Redivivus. Wendell D. Garrett, 1971.

Thomas Jefferson: An Intimate History. Fawn M. Brodie, 1974.

The Inner Jefferson: Portrait of a Grieving Optimist. Andrew Burstein, 1995

American Sphinx: The Character of Thomas Jefferson. Joseph J. Ellis, 1997.

DOMESTIC LIFE AND MONTICELLO

The Domestic Life of Thomas Jefferson. Sarah N. Randolph, 1871; reissued 1978.

Jefferson's Monticello. William Howard Adams, 1983.

The Garden and Farm Books of Thomas Jefferson. Robert C. Baron, ed., 1987.

The Worlds of Thomas Jefferson at Monticello. Susan R. Stein, 1993.
Archaeology at Monticello. William M. Kelso, 1997.

THE UNIVERSITY OF VIRGINIA

Mr. Jefferson's University: A History. Virginius Dabney, 1981.
Thomas Jefferson's Academical Village. Richard Guy Wilson, ed., 1993.
The University of Virginia: A Pictorial History. Susan Tyler Hitchcock, 1999.
The Corner: A History of Student Life at the University of Virginia. Coy Barefoot, 2001.

THE SALLY HEMINGS DEBATE

Thomas Jefferson and Sally Hemings: An American Controversy. Annette Gordon-Reed, 1997.
"Jefferson Fathered Slave's Last Child," *Nature,* Eugene A. Foster, et al., November 5, 1998.
The Jefferson–Hemings Myth: An American Travesty. Eyler Coates, Sr., ed., 2001.
The Thomas Jefferson Memorial Foundation maintains a comprehensive collection of material related to this debate at its website, *www.monticello.org*
The PBS investigative series *Frontline* aired a superb study of the story in April 2000. A detailed companion website for that broadcast can be located at *www.pbs.org/wgbh/pages/frontline*

SLAVERY AND RACE

American Slavery, American Freedom. Edmund S. Morgan, 1975; 1995.
The Wolf by the Ears: Thomas Jefferson and Slavery. John Chester Miller, 1991.
Slavery at Monticello. Lucia Stanton, 1996.
Free Some Day: The African-American Families of Monticello. Lucia Stanton, 2001.

POLITICAL CAREER AND PHILOSOPHY

Thomas Jefferson as Political Leader. Dumas Malone, 1963.

Jefferson and the Presidency: Leadership in the Young Republic. Robert Johnstone, Jr., 1978.

The Adams–Jefferson Letters: The Complete Correspondence. Lester J. Cappon, ed., 1988.

Empire of Liberty: The Statecraft of Thomas Jefferson. Robert W. Tucker and David C. Hendrickson, 1992.

Jeffersonian Legacies. Peter S. Onuf, ed., 1993.

The Constitutional Thought of Thomas Jefferson. David N. Mayer, 1995.

America Afire: Jefferson, Adams, and the Revolutionary Election of 1800. Bernard A. Weisberger, 2000.

Founding Brothers: The Revolutionary Generation. Joseph J. Ellis, 2000.

SCHOLARLY ARTICLES

"The Scholar's Jefferson," Peter S. Onuf. *William and Mary Quarterly* (1993).

"A Poet, A Planter, And a Nation of Farmers," Richard Lyman Bushman. *Journal of the Early Republic* (Spring 1999).

"Thomas Jefferson's Changing Reputation as Author of the Declaration of Independence: The First Fifty Years," Robert M.S. McDonald. *Journal of the Early Republic* (Summer 1999).

"The Seductions of Thomas Jefferson," Andrew Burstein. *Journal of the Early Republic* (Fall 1999).

A Forum regarding Thomas Jefferson's Letter to the Danbury Baptists and the Wall of Separation Between Church and State, *William and Mary Quarterly* (October 1999). Includes articles by James H. Hutton, Robert M. O'Neil, Thomas E. Buckley, Edwin S. Gaustad, Daniel L. Dreisback, Issac Kramnick, and R. Laurence Moore.

"The Jeffersonian Triumph and American Exceptionalism," John M. Murrin. *Journal of the Early Republic* (Spring, 2000).

VIDEO

Lewis & Clark: The Journey of the Corps of Discovery. Ken Burns, 1997.

Thomas Jefferson: A Film by Ken Burns, 1997.

WORLD WIDE WEB

Monticello—informative site, home to The Thomas Jefferson Memorial Foundation and the International Center for Jefferson Studies.
www.monticello.org

Thomas Jefferson Online Resources at the University of Virginia—one of the best places on the Web to begin learning about Thomas Jefferson; includes links to many thousands of pages of original writings, bibliographies, and online exhibitions.
etext.virginia.edu/jefferson

Thomas Jefferson On Politics & Government: Quotations from the Writings of Thomas Jefferson. Edited by Eyler Coates, Sr.—an extremely comprehensive searchable site with numerous links.
etext.virginia.edu/jefferson/quotations

The Thomas Jefferson Papers at the Library of Congress—a massive searchable site with thousands of original writings.
memory.loc.gov/ammem/mtjhtml/mtjhome.html

ACKNOWLEDGMENTS

I am tremendously grateful to Lucia Stanton, Senior Research Historian at the Thomas Jefferson Memorial Foundation, for her gracious assistance in my research. I would also like to thank Bo Short of the American Leadership Foundation, as well as Eyler Coates, Charles Frohman, and Salvatore Salvaggio for their input. Though I was fortunate to receive help from many, I accept full responsibility for any factual errors in this book.

Thanks as well to Scott Moyers, Daniel Greenberg, Gary Brozek, and Amanda Patten for helping to make this project happen. I am of course particularly thankful to my family for their encouragement and support. And to my wife, Alison—my love, my best friend, my partner on this amazing adventure—thank you from the bottom of my heart.

INDEX

Coy Barefoot is a recognized expert on Thomas Jefferson and the author of *The Quixtar Revolution*, a *Wall Street Journal* business bestseller. He is a guest lecturer at the University of Virginia and a chairman of the Historic Resources Task Force, a group that works with the Thomas Jefferson Memorial Foundation to preserve and promote the history of Charlottesville, Virginia. He lives in Oneonta, New York.